When we see in Scripture the dying love of our Savior on the cross, pouring out His life for hell-worthy sinners, we should exclaim with the apostle John, "What manner of love is this!" The twenty-four hours between the Passover meal in the upper room and the death of Christ on the cross of Calvary are indeed the most significant twenty-four hours in history. Brother Chris Anderson—a gifted hymn-writer as well as a devotional writer—helps us slow down during these twenty-four hours, as do the four evangelists, to consider the upper room discourse, the high-priestly prayer of Christ, and the substitutionary atonement of our Lord on the cross in His journey from Gethsemane to Gabbatha to Golgotha. By pointing us back to the love of the Triune God, revealing the humanity and divinity of the Lord Jesus, and calling sinners to embrace Christ as freely offered in the gospel, these thirty-one meditations reveal the One Who alone can give us everlasting life through the gospel. Find here medicine for the weary soul!

> **Joel Beeke,** Chancellor and Professor of Systematic Theology and Homiletics, Puritan Reformed Theological Seminary, and Pastor of Heritage Reformed Congregation, Grand Rapids, Michigan

I have read *Sundown to Sundown* with profit to my soul. The last day of Jesus' earthly life makes a sobering journey. Chris Anderson has obviously traveled the road many times as a careful observer of the sufferings of our Lord. In this book he guides us to confront the most sobering moments in sacred history. I recommend the book as a series of devotional readings with a chapter for each day before Good Friday.

> **Kevin Bauder,** Research Professor of Systematic Theology, Central Baptist Theological Seminary, and Pastor of Bible Baptist Church, East Bethel, Minnesota

We live in a culture that moves at an unrelenting pace, often conditioning us to do the same—leaving little time to practice the lost art of meditation. But Christian meditation is distinct from the emptying practices of other world religions. Instead of clearing the mind of everything, biblical meditation calls us to fill our hearts and minds with the truths, promises, and beauty of God as revealed in His Word. In this insightful book, Chris Anderson provides a focused guide to help us meditate on Christ's work in His final hours before and on the cross. As you walk through these reflections, your heart will be drawn to the depth of His suffering and the greatness of His love. This is a book you'll want to add to your library.

    Josh Buice, Pastor of Pray's Mill Baptist Church, Douglasville, Georgia, Founder and President of G3 Ministries, and Assistant Professor of Preaching at Grace Bible Theological Seminary, Conway, Arkansas

Chris Anderson helps us reflect on the final hours of Jesus' life—the redemptive work that changed everything for us. This devotional is an invitation to find hope in the midst of sorrow. Each day's reading is paired with a beautiful hymn, echoing the themes of the Scripture and inviting us into a deeper, more personal worship experience. These reflections will nourish your soul and guide you closer to the heart of Christ. As you meditate each day on His last hours, your appreciation for Christ's cross will deepen. *Sundown to Sundown* will leave you moved by the grace of the One Who gave His all for you.

    Josh Crokett, President of Bob Jones University

Chris Anderson

SUNDOWN to SUNDOWN

*Meditations on
the Twenty-Four Hours
Preceding Jesus'
Death*

©2025 All Rights Reserved.

Sundown to Sundown: Meditations on the Twenty-Four Hours Preceding Jesus' Death
Copyright ©2025 by Chris Anderson
All rights reserved. This book or parts thereof may not be reproduced in any form, stored in any retrieval system, or transmitted in any form by any means—electronic, mechanical, photocopy, recording, or otherwise—without prior written permission of the publisher, except as provided by United States of America copyright law. For permission requests, write to connect@churchworksmedia.com.

Unless otherwise indicated, Scripture quotations are from the ESV Bible (*The Holy Bible, English Standard Version*), copyright ©2001 by Crossway, a publishing ministry of Good News Publishers. Used by permission. All rights reserved.

Thank you to RitaE (Pixabay) for the cover image.
Used by permission.

Published by Church Works Media
FIRST EDITION 2025
Editing by Abby Huffstutler and Paul Keew
Cover design and layout by Joe Tyrpak

ISBN 979-8-9873274-7-0 (paperback)
churchworksmedia.com

To the Lord Jesus Christ,
"Who loved me and gave Himself for me"
(Galatians 2:20)

TABLE OF CONTENTS

FOREWORD ... 7

INTRODUCTION ... 9

DAY 1 — JESUS' LOVE FOR HIS OWN ... 13

DAY 2 — JESUS' NEW COMMAND ... 19

DAY 3 — JESUS AND THE FATHER ... 23

DAY 4 — JESUS' APPROACHING DEPARTURE— AND RETURN ... 27

DAY 5 — JESUS' PROMISE OF THE HOLY SPIRIT ... 31

DAY 6 — JESUS, THE LIFE-GIVING VINE ... 35

DAY 7 — JESUS' DISCIPLES AND THE HOSTILE WORLD ... 39

DAY 8 — JESUS' GLORY IN THE CROSS ... 43

DAY 9 — JESUS, THE NEW PASSOVER ... 47

DAY 10 — JESUS' FRAIL FRIENDS ... 51

DAY 11 — JESUS' HIGH-PRIESTLY PRAYER ... 55

DAY 12 — JESUS' AGONY IN THE GARDEN ... 61

DAY 13 — JESUS' BETRAYAL AND ARREST ... 65

DAY 14 — JESUS BEFORE THE SANHEDRIN ... 69

DAY 15 — JESUS' MOCKERY AND BEATINGS ... 73

DAY 16 — JESUS' POWER AND PETER'S WEAKNESS ... 79

DAY 17 — JESUS' BETRAYER ... 83

DAY 18 — JESUS BEFORE HEROD ... 87

DAY 19 — JESUS BEFORE PILATE ... 91

DAY 20 — JESUS AND THE FRENZIED MOB ... 97

DAY 21 — JESUS' JOURNEY TO GOLGOTHA ... 101

DAY 22 — JESUS' CRUCIFIXION ... 107

DAY 23 — JESUS' PRAYER: "FATHER, FORGIVE THEM" ... 111

DAY 24 — JESUS' MERCY: "TODAY YOU WILL BE WITH ME IN PARADISE" ... 117

DAY 25 — JESUS' COMPASSION: "WOMAN, BEHOLD YOUR SON" ... 123

DAY 26 — JESUS' ABANDONMENT: "WHY HAVE YOU FORSAKEN ME?" ... 127

DAY 27 — JESUS' HUMANITY: "I THIRST" ... 133

DAY 28 — JESUS' TRIUMPH: "IT IS FINISHED" ... 137

DAY 29 — JESUS' FAITH: "FATHER, INTO YOUR HANDS I COMMEND MY SPIRIT" ... 141

DAY 30 — JESUS' POWER, EVEN IN DEATH ... 145

DAY 31 — JESUS' BURIAL—AND REST ... 151

ACKNOWLEDGMENTS ... 157

HYMNS ... 159

BIBLIOGRAPHY ... 165

FOREWORD

Chris Anderson loves to preach, and he never preaches with more passion than when he preaches on the cross. As Chris' full-time associate from 2005–2012, I had an up-close view of the way his preaching on Christ's passion transformed him and our congregation. In April–June 2007 he fed two precious chapters, Matthew 26–27, to Tri–County Bible Church, Madison, Ohio. As that series wrapped up, I encouraged Chris to develop his study in writing. On Good Friday, April 2, 2010, we delivered a small devotional titled *Sundown to Sundown* to attendees at our annual Passion Service, which included several other churches in Northeast Ohio.

Since that time, I've encouraged Chris to expand that little booklet into a fuller devotional we could publish together through Church Works Media. Thankfully, he has now done so, adding extensive work on John 13–17.

His ten weeks in Matthew 26–27 kept his attention on the substitutionary death of Jesus, and his attention has never left that topic. He has become deeply convinced that the center of the gospel must be the center of the Christian life, the center of the church's life and testimony, and the center of preaching. And Chris lives this conviction. He personally delights in the gospel, feeds his soul on the gospel, fights his sin with the gospel, ministers the gospel to his family, muses on the gospel day and night, and talks about it in almost every conversation.

In our early years together, these gospel musings resulted in several hymn texts which have well served many churches' corporate worship of the Lord Jesus. Chris has continued writing hymn lyrics on Christ's finished work. So, just as I included a portion from one of his hymns in each devotional in the first *Sundown to Sundown* booklet in 2010, we've done so in this copy as well.

I am delighted to recommend—and, as the lead designer, to present—this devotional booklet to you. I pray that it will be used by the Lord to inflame your love for Christ Jesus, Who "made himself nothing" and "humbled himself by becoming obedient to the point of death, even death on a cross" (Philippians 2:7–8).

Joe Tyrpak
Madison, Ohio
2025

INTRODUCTION

The most remarkable twenty-four hours in history began with a feast which marked the passing of the Old Covenant and the dawning of the New—just after sunset.

That day like no other—*sundown to sundown*—included Jesus' time with the disciples in the upper room, Jesus' high-priestly prayer, Jesus' agony in Gethsemane, Jesus' betrayal by Judas, Jesus' abandonment by the disciples, Jesus' arrest and trials through the night, and ultimately, Jesus' crucifixion and cries from the cross.

Whereas the four Gospels spend sixty-six chapters on the first three years of Jesus' ministry, they decelerate significantly during its final week. Nearly a third of the chapters in the Gospels focus on the last week before Jesus' death. And the biblical record slows to a snail's pace during these final twenty-four hours, zooming in and allowing us to marvel at the mystery of Jesus' suffering.

This means that *thirteen chapters*—almost fifteen percent of the Gospels—are taken up with this *single day*. John Stott points out, "John's Gospel has justly been described as having two parts, 'the book of the signs' and 'the book of the Passion,' since John spends an almost equal amount of time on each." He further notes that even the resurrected Christ focused His teaching primarily on the significance of His death—"not the living but the giving of his life."[1]

Jesus' public ministry crescendoed in a remarkable way during His final week. He had entered Jerusalem in triumph, presenting Himself as the Messiah to the multitudes crammed into the Holy City for the Passover (Matthew 21:1–11). He had wept over the city, His chest heaving as He mourned over the Jews' rejection of Him and their approaching judgement (Luke 19:41–44). He had embarrassed several waves of insincere questioners with His infinite wisdom (Matthew 22:15–46). His final teaching sessions, focused on His future return and reign, were thunderous (Matthew 24–25).

---

1 John Stott, *The Cross of Christ* (Downers Grove, IL: IVP Books, 2006), 37–38.

Then came the final twenty-four hours. And everything. Slowed. Down.

It isn't just the Gospels that focus our attention on Jesus' final hours. The entire New Testament is a commentary on the cross. William Evans writes, "The New Testament is the Book of the Cross. Cut the New Testament anywhere, and it bleeds. Through every page runs the scarlet cord of redemption."[2]

The Old Testament is surprisingly cross-centered as well. W. A. Criswell explains:

> At least seventy-five percent of the prophecies concerning Christ in the Old Testament were fulfilled *during this week!* ... It seemed that every step in His judgment and crucifixion was described accurately in the Old Testament and fulfilled exactly as it was described.[3]

Do you see? Do you understand the significance of this single day?

With unmistakable wonder, the four Gospels tether our attention to Jesus' last day. Those precious hours were spent first with His friends and then with His foes—teaching, then suffering.

Jesus' last twenty-four hours began with unrivaled teaching.

Jesus began His final fleeting hours with the twelve—then the eleven—not the multitudes. Those few hours are remarkable for their tenderness. As His own suffering approached, He spoke to His disciples intimately and encouragingly, preparing them for all that lay ahead. Although I've often described the Sermon on the Mount as the greatest sermon ever preached, the upper-room discourse may change my mind. Jesus' teaching and prayer in John 13–17 changed the world.

Jesus' last twenty-four hours ended with unrivaled suffering.

In Gethsemane, following a season of agonizing prayer with the Father, Jesus was turned over to His foes. For the rest of the night,

---

[2] William Evans, *Epochs in the Life of Christ* (New York, NY: Fleming H. Revell Company, 1916), 126.

[3] W. A. Criswell, *Preaching on the Life of Christ: Sermons on the Epochs in the Life of Christ* (Grand Rapids, MI: Zondervan Publishing House, 1958), 78, 83.

they berated and bullied Him through multiple trials and tortures. As morning dawned, they culminated their butchery with a barbaric crucifixion. Jesus' suffering wouldn't end until His lifeless body was taken down from the cross and laid in a borrowed tomb.

The Bible passages which draw our attention to the Lord Jesus are holy ground. The upper room is the ultimate encapsulation of divine wisdom. And the cross is the ultimate expression of divine love. Jerry Bridges writes,

> There is no doubt that the most convincing evidence of God's love in all of Scripture is His giving His Son to die for our sins.... If we want proof of God's love for us, then we must look first at the Cross where God offered up His Son as a sacrifice for our sins. Calvary is the one objective, absolute, irrefutable proof of God's love for us.[4]

If you pay attention, Jesus' last twenty-four hours will change you. I've experienced it. This book took shape during a particularly challenging time in my life. Looking to Jesus' words and wounds, day after difficult day, nourished my soul. I pray that the same will be true for you, and that you will never be the same. Grace.

Chris Anderson
Grayson, Georgia
2025

> *We were scattered, lost and battered—*
> *Head-strong sheep gone astray.*
> *Ever roaming, ever groaning,*
> *Hell-bent on our own way.*
> *Jesus, Shepherd, loving Shepherd,*
> *Sent from heaven to earth—*
> *You have sought us, found and brought us*
> *Safely into Your church.*

---

[4] Jerry Bridges, *Trusting God* (Colorado Springs, CO: NavPress, 2008), 146.

We were filthy, gravely guilty;
Justice called for our blood.
Death was looming; hell was fuming—
Who could save us from God?
Jesus, Shepherd, bleeding Shepherd,
By Your wounds we are purged.
Lamb, unblemished, You have finished
All for love for Your church!

You have made us and have saved us
At an infinite price.
Now we're praying that the straying
Will, like us, turn to Christ.
Jesus, Shepherd, saving Shepherd,
We have joined in Your search.
As You found us, now astound us
By expanding Your church! [5]

---

5 Chris Anderson and Matt Taylor, "Jesus, Shepherd" (The Wilds, 2023).

DAY 1

JESUS' LOVE FOR HIS OWN
John 13

The disciples gathered to observe the Passover feast with Jesus at sundown. If there were ever a moment in Jesus' brief life when He might have selfishly insisted on solitude, this was the night. Our Lord was mere hours away from betrayal, beatings, and a bloody death. A night of quiet contemplation was in order, it would seem. Or perhaps even a night of doting and encouragement by His friends before His fast-approaching agonies.

And yet, Jesus spent His final night serving His disciples in the upper room. He would teach them. He would warn them. He would pray for them, and for us. He would even tolerate their dullness, responding with patient gentleness rather than exasperation as they bickered amongst themselves.

In the words of John 13:1, "He loved them to the end." To the end of His life. To the end of His mission. To the end of His crucifixion. To a measure so absolute that no more love was even possible.

As day dimmed into the Passover night, Jesus did something remarkable. Rather than receiving the service of others—as He had when Mary anointed His head a few days earlier (Matthew 26:6–13)—Jesus took upon Himself the most menial and demeaning of tasks. He took off the garments over which the soldiers would gamble a few hours later, clothed Himself with a towel, and washed the disciples' feet (John 13:3–5). The condescension is staggering—a small picture of the downward spiral described in Philippians 2:5–8.

Remarkably, it seems that He washed even the devil Judas' feet (John 13:2). He loved *even Judas* to the end, though it was love unrequited.

Jesus' actions were filled with significance. The washing of feet is no ordinance of the church. But it was a holy act. It was one of the most remarkable moments in a ministry marked by miracles. It was a work of art, a picture of selflessness, a living and breathing sermon.

Jesus washed the feet of His disciples to serve them and love them.
Washing the disciples' feet was no mere object lesson. We mustn't lose the wonder of what Jesus *did* in our rush to get to the "moral of the story." Jesus served them because He is the ultimate Servant. Yes, He was their Lord and Master, as He would remind them (John 13:13–14). He was fully cognizant that He was coequal with the Father and Spirit, that "the Father had given all things into his hands" (John 13:3). Nevertheless, He served the disciples just as He had served lepers, cripples, and harlots throughout His earthly ministry. Before we see an example to follow, we must savor the beauty and benevolence and breathtaking love of our Savior. He washed their feet. Hard stop.

Jesus washed the feet of His disciples to teach them to serve and love one another.
After Jesus washed the disciples' feet, He commanded these men to follow His example by serving one another (John 13:15, 17)—likely not in ritual washings, but in a life of humble service that notices and addresses the needs of others. Matthew Henry writes, "When we see our Master serving, we cannot but see how ill it becomes us to be domineering."[6]

The disciples didn't yet get it. They were still annoyingly ambitious. Admiring Jesus' humility is much easier than adopting Jesus' humility. We, like the disciples, are infuriatingly selfish. But this lesson *would* eventually take and become a reality for them, as we see in the remarkable transformation of the disciples after the outpouring of the Spirit.

---

6 Matthew Henry, *Matthew Henry's Commentary on the Whole Bible: Complete and Unabridged in One Volume* (Peabody, MA: Hendrickson Publishers, 1994), 2008.

Finally, Jesus washed the feet of His disciples to show that He had washed their souls. D. A. Carson notes that the foot washing was "symbolic of spiritual cleansing."[7] Jesus had come to earth to cleanse the disciples' spiritual filth, just as He was washing from them the grime of the day. So the foot washing was a metaphor. In a typical mingling of virtue and vice, Peter initially refused to allow Jesus to wash his feet (John 13:6, 8). We can appreciate Peter's sense of propriety; the other disciples appear to have accepted Jesus' grand gesture without any such scruples, which may have been even worse. Peter at least had the humility to feel awkward.

But Peter was misguided. (Stop me if you've heard this before.) As Jesus washed His disciples' feet, He deftly moved the conversation from the physical to the spiritual, by now with some predictability. And upon learning from Jesus that cleansing was a condition of fellowship, Peter asked Jesus to wash *his entire body* (John 13:8–9)! I admire that. I relate to the bumbling sincerity of Peter. He's all in.

But note Jesus' response: He explained that He used the image of foot washing to describe daily spiritual maintenance (John 13:10). True, deep spiritual cleansing—the full-body "bath" of your soul, what we sometimes call getting "saved"—happens when we *initially* turn from sin to Christ. It happens in a moment, and it is irrevocable. But because walking through this sin-filled world inevitably gets us splattered with the world's muck, we need regular washing, too— daily confession, ongoing repentance, and the blessing of *relational* forgiveness (1 John 1:9; 2:1–2). Based on our original salvation— better, based on Christ's finished work!—we depend on our Savior to continually forgive us and cleanse us from all unrighteousness so that we may have unhindered fellowship with Him.

It's a beautiful lesson. But it's also a staggering affirmation of the eleven, with only Judas described as still lost in sin (John 13:10, 18– 19, 21–30). Notice how Jesus affirmed the disciples' faith, frail as it

---

7   D. A. Carson, *The Gospel According to John* (Grand Rapids, MI: William B. Eerdmans Publishing Company, 1991), 458.

was: "You are clean" (John 13:10). *You are clean.* The commendation staggers almost as much as Jesus' condescension. Fully aware that they would argue about their greatness in mere minutes, and fully aware that they would forsake Him in mere hours, Jesus assured the eleven that they were indeed forgiven. They had believed in Him. They had been cleansed from their sins. They would be preserved, and even their heartbreaking failures of that tragic night would be washed away. That's astonishing grace.

Jesus loved the disciples to the end. They were His own. Feeble as they were, they were clean—all because of Jesus. *Are you?*

Keeper of the withered reed,
You have wept o'er human need;
Guardian of the smold'ring flame,
You restored the blind and lame.
Move Your church to be like You—
Help us do what You would do.
Help us do what You would do.

Lifter of the leper's woe,
You have loved the poor and low;
Friend of those without a friend,
You bowed down to soothe and mend.
Move Your church to love like Christ—
Help us welcome the despised.
Help us welcome the despised.

> *Savior of the sinful soul*
> *You were pierced to make us whole;*
> *Lamb of God Who took our place*
> *You were cursed to give us grace.*
> *Move Your church with gospel truth—*
> *Help us bring the lost to You.*
> *Help us bring the lost to You.*[8]

---

[8] Chris Anderson and Richard A. Nichols, "The Love of Christ" (Church Works Media, 2015).

DAY 2

JESUS' NEW COMMAND
John 13:34–35

John 13 begins with Jesus' command for the disciples to *serve* one another. John 13 ends with Jesus' command for the disciples to *love* one another:

> A new commandment I give to you, that you love one another: just as I have loved you, you also are to love one another. By this all people will know that you are my disciples, if you have love for one another. (John 13:34–35)

Once again, the timing of Jesus' words highlights their importance. Mere hours away from His own agonies, He ensured that His disciples would love and be loved—not only by Him, but by each other. As He prepared for His approaching departure, He readied them to look out for each other in His absence, first in mutual service and then in mutual love.

It's significant—and perhaps a bit puzzling—that Jesus called His charge to love one another a *new* command. Throughout the Old Testament, God gave His people two foundational commands: to love Him supremely (Deuteronomy 6:5) and to love one another as themselves (Leviticus 19:18). These commands—the first and great commandment and the one akin to it—are a summary of the entire Old Testament Law and prophets (Matthew 22:35–40). Since that's the case, in what sense was Jesus' command *new*?

In this version of the "love one another" command, the *extreme measure* of the love was new. Whereas the Old Testament commanded God's people to love each other as they loved themselves, Jesus raised the bar. They were no longer to love like the best of men, or even like they selfishly looked out for themselves. Now, they were to love *like Him*, "just as I have loved you" (John 13:34).

That's infinite love. It's love "to the end" (John 13:1). It's selfless love: "I lay down my life for the sheep" (John 10:15). It's a supernatural love: "As the Father has loved me, so have I loved you" (John 15:9). It's a sacrificial love: "This is my commandment, that you love one another as I have loved you. Greater love has no one than this, that someone lay down his life for his friends" (John 15:12–13).

It is an underserved, undeterred, unrelenting love, even when we have earned nothing but wrath: "In this is love, not that we have loved God but that he loved us and sent his Son to be the propitiation for our sins" (1 John 4:10). It is this divine love, originating in God Himself, that is the measure of how we are to love each other. And so the apostle John follows up 1 John 4:10 with this application: "Beloved, if God so loved us, we also ought to love one another" (1 John 4:11).

Jesus first issued this life-changing command in John 13:34–35. But He repeated it throughout the upper-room discourse (John 15:9, 12, 13, 17). And He prayed that we would love each other in His high-priestly prayer (John 17:26). Please don't miss this. Even as Jesus' own ruin loomed, He was preoccupied with a singular burden: that Christians should love other Christians.

Jesus taught that this Christ-like love for other hard-to-love Christians is the very mark of our faith—the ultimate apologetic, the way unbelievers will know that we are His disciples (John 13:35). That means that there's an evangelistic consequence to our love. A watching world can't help but notice it when otherwise dissimilar people *love* each other instead of *rivaling* each other. There's a fragrance of Jesus about such love.

But it's not only the world who will know that we are Christians by our love. We *ourselves* will know that we are genuine believers by our love for fellow Christians. The apostle John—the eyewitness recorder of Jesus' words in the upper room—repeatedly reminds us in his first letter that love for other Christians is one of the distinguishing marks of a genuine believer (1 John 2:10; 3:10–11, 14, 16–18, 23; 4:7, 8, 11–12, 16–18, 19–21; 5:1–2).

To put a sharper point on it, John repeatedly tells us that those who don't obey Jesus' new and essential command are still lost in their sins.

> Whoever does not practice righteousness is not of God, nor is the one who does not love his brother. (1 John 3:10)
>
> Whoever does not love abides in death. (1 John 3:14)
>
> But if anyone has the world's goods and sees his brother in need, yet closes his heart against him, how does God's love abide in him? (1 John 3:17)
>
> Anyone who does not love does not know God, because God is love. (1 John 4:8)
>
> If anyone says, "I love God," and hates his brother, he is a liar; for he who does not love his brother whom he has seen cannot love God whom he has not seen. (1 John 4:20)

Jesus commanded us to love each other. He showed us how. He made our mutual love a proof of our faith—even a *test* of our faith. And He commands us throughout the New Testament, with almost exhausting redundancy, to grow in this capstone of all Christian virtues.

It's that important. God help us.

> *I love Your Church, Your holy bride*
> *Whom You have saved and unified.*
> *May love abound within our church*
> *And spread from us to all the earth.*
>
> *Teach me to love as You love me—*
> *To give with generosity.*
> *And as I share the things I've earned,*
> *My gifts are but Your love, returned.*[9]

~

---

[9] Chris Anderson and Richard A. Nichols, "Your Love Returned" (Church Works Media, 2019).

I love the church, my fam'ly o'er the earth—
Sinners estranged, made one through second birth.
In selfless love Christ claimed us as His own,
And that same love from each to each is shown.

May Christ be praised: "Preeminent! Adored!"
I love Your church because I love her Lord.[10]

---

10 Chris Anderson and Greg Habegger, "I Love the Church" (Church Works Media, 2009).

DAY

3

JESUS AND THE FATHER
John 13–17

The Gospel of John constantly draws our attention to the unique relationship between God the Father and the God the Son. We learn that Jesus is coequal and coeternal with the Father. Jesus reveals the Father. He is one with the Father, was sent by the Father, always pleases the Father, and so on. It comes as no surprise, then, that Jesus' final hours before His crucifixion were spent talking about—and talking *to*—His heavenly Father.

We often think of Trinitarian doctrine as one of the difficulties of biblical orthodoxy. We know it's true and necessary ... but *ouch*, it's hard to wrap our minds around it, much less defend it. But that perspective is skewed. Rightly understood, the doctrine of the Trinity is exceptionally encouraging and practical. Sinclair Ferguson writes,

> When his disciples were about to have the world collapse in on them, our Lord spent so much time in the upper room speaking to them about the mystery of the Trinity. If anything could underline the necessity of Trinitarianism for practical Christianity, that must surely be it![11]

Jesus anticipated returning to His Father (John 13:1, 14:12, 28; 16:10, 28; 17:11).

As soon as we are ushered into the upper room, we read that Jesus was pondering His upcoming departure. He was going "to the Father" (John 13:1). He wasn't just going to the cross, or the tomb, or even to heaven. He was going back to the Father.

In one of the Gospel's tenderest scenes, Jesus prayed in John 17:5 about His return to His relinquished glory and to His Father's

---

11 Quoted in Robert Letham, *The Holy Trinity: In Scripture, History, Theology, and Worship* (Phillipsburg, NJ: P&R Publishing, 2019), xxvii.

intimate presence: "And now, Father, glorify me in your own presence with the glory that I had with you before the world existed." Christ would endure the Father's excruciating *absence* during the crucifixion. But He relished the sweet reunion that would be His reward for those miserable hours. "The joy that was set before Him," to quote Hebrews 12:2, included His reunion with the Father. This expectancy buoyed our Savior on this darkest of nights.

We will never understand Jesus' mission to earth unless we gaze, wide-eyed, at the love between the Father and the Son. Neglecting this leads us to a perverse understanding of the cross, as though it were "divine child abuse"—the Father's calloused trading of a perfect Son for undeserving rebels. The cross was certainly a display of divine love for the sin-sick world, and at a great expense (Romans 5:8). But it was even more so a ministry of divine love between the Father and the Son (John 10:17; 17:24), agreed upon in eternity past.

Richard Bauckham explains: "The love between the Father and the Son is the deepest dimension not only of the Gospel's understanding of God, but also of the Gospel's soteriology."[12]

The exchange of love between the three Members of the Godhead is remarkable. But there's more.

Jesus invited His disciples to share in the love of His Father (John 14:21, 23; 15:9–10; 16:27; 17:21).

Jesus' high-priestly prayer in John 17 will receive our full attention later in this study. It is astonishing for many reasons. But most shocking to me is that Jesus invites His disciples to share in the perfect, selfless love which the Father, Son, and Spirit have enjoyed among Themselves for all eternity.[13] The concept defies comprehension. It should take your breath away. We don't experience only the overflow of divine love, imitating it or reflecting it. We are invited into our triune God's love as *participants*.

---

12 Richard Bauckham, "The Trinity and the Gospel of John" in *The Essential Trinity: New Testament Foundations and Practical Relevance*, eds. Brandon D. Crowe and Carl R. Trueman (Phillipsburg, NJ: P&R Publishing, 2016), 112.

13 If you've not yet read Michael Reeves's book on the Trinity, rectify that as soon as possible. Michael Reeves, *Delighting in the Trinity: An Introduction to the Christian Faith* (Downers Grove, IL: IVP Academic, 2012).

Again, Bauckham is helpful:

> Looking back from the vantage point of the conclusion of Jesus' prayer [in John 17], we could say that the whole story of salvation that the Gospel tells stems from the love between the Father and the Son and has as its goal the inclusion of humans within this loving relationship.[14]

If that doesn't overwhelm you, you're not paying attention. The apostle John, who recorded Jesus' words in the upper room, continued to revel in this mystery decades later. He writes, "See what kind of love the Father has given to us, that we should be called children of God; and so we are" (1 John 3:1).

> *The Father looks on me and sees*
> *Not what I was or am;*
> *He views the righteousness of Christ,*
> *And not my cursèd sin.*
> *The Father looks and pities me;*
> *He knows that I am dust.*
> *He treats me not as I deserve,*
> *But as though I were just.*
>
> *The Father looks for me with hope,*
> *For me, His wayward son.*
> *I stand afar, detained by shame;*
> *He cries for joy and runs!*
> *The Father looks on me and smiles,*
> *For it is Christ He sees;*
> *"This is my own belovèd son,*
> *In whom I am well pleased."*[15]

∼

---

14 Bauckham, 112.

15 Chris Anderson and Rebekah Holden, "The Father Looks on Me" (Church Works Media, 2015).

DAY 4

JESUS' APPROACHING DEPARTURE—AND RETURN

John 14:1–6; 16:22

Try to imagine that you're one of the disciples. You've gathered with Jesus in the upper room. It's another Passover meal, which you've experienced every year of your life. But everything about this one feels different. You've been astonished by Jesus' selfless act of washing your feet—an act that somehow made you feel both honored and ashamed. Now you're listening to Jesus' words. And there are *so many words*!

He commands you to serve each other. He commands you to love each other. He says that one of you will betray Him. That catches your attention! And it sparks some self-doubt. *Could it be you?*

Jesus goes on to speak of His Father, of His Spirit, of the hostile world, of the privilege to pray in His name (whatever that means). It's all overwhelming. You're trying to take it all in, convinced by Jesus' intensity that these lessons are vitally important. But it's already been a long day, climaxing a long week and, frankly, three long years. You can't keep up.

And yet, one repeated theme from Jesus' talk keeps coming up with frightening frequency. At first you assume that you must have misheard—but there it is again. Jesus keeps talking about *leaving*. It's clear that He doesn't want you to miss this point. It feels like He's getting you ready to carry on in His absence. But that seems so out of place—so defeatist—especially just a few days after the excitement of His triumphal entry into Jerusalem. Just when things are getting good, Jesus is fixated on His departure. What gives?

You wonder if it's just you, but a fellow disciple nudges you: "What does He mean when He says, 'A little while, and you will not see me?' or 'I am going to the Father'?" (John 16:17–18). Imagine the murmuring: "I'm lost. He's not seriously going away, is He? This is a metaphor, right? Maybe Peter or John can talk Him out of this."

But you're not mistaken. Jesus keeps talking about His departure. He's leaving.

> I go to prepare a place for you. (John 14:2)
>
> And if I go…. (John 14:3)
>
> And you know the way to where I am going. (John 14:4)
>
> Yet a little while and the world will see me no more. (John 14:19)
>
> I am going away…. I am going to the Father. (John 14:28)
>
> I am going to him who sent me, and none of you asks me, "Where are you going?" But because I have said these things to you, sorrow has filled your heart. (John 16:5–6)
>
> A little while, and you will see me no longer. (John 16:16, 19)
>
> I am leaving the world and going to the Father. (John 16:28)

A pall hovers over the room. Reality sets in. As Jesus Himself said, sorrow has filled your heart (John 16:6), mingled with confusion, dread, even some anger as you absorb what feels like utter abandonment.

And yet, as you strain to clear your head and focus on Jesus' words, it dawns on you that you're hearing only half the story. Yes, He says He's leaving. But He also says He's going to *return*—not only to be with you on Earth, but to take you to be *with Him in heaven*. Can that be right? Could it be that the prize for which you've endured three long years isn't an earthly kingdom, but a kingdom in heaven? Is your hope deferred? Is your best life later?

Jesus' words on this point couldn't be clearer.

DAY 4 — JESUS' APPROACHING DEPARTURE— AND RETURN

Let not your hearts be troubled. Believe in God; believe also in me. In my Father's house are many rooms. If it were not so, would I have told you that I go to prepare a place for you? And if I go and prepare a place for you, I will come again and will take you to myself, that where I am you may be also. And you know the way to where I am going.

Thomas said to him, "Lord, we do not know where you are going. How can we know the way?"

Jesus said to him, "I am the way, and the truth, and the life. No one comes to the Father except through me." (John 14:1–6)

Many of us know this text so well that we take it for granted. Jesus' comfort of the disciples throughout this night rested primarily on two truths, both of them tied to the Trinity. He promised to *send them* the Spirit. But He also promised to *take them to* the Father.

Jesus assures us that His Father's house has ample room for us. But His invitation, generous as it is, comes with a condition: *Only He can take us to the Father.* John 14:6 provides what is perhaps the clearest gospel message from the lips of Jesus. Access to the Father comes through Christ alone; He is *the* way to God, not *a* way. If you don't go to God through Him, You don't go at all. There's no room for debate—no quarter for pluralism or tolerance or ecumenism. It's Jesus or nothing. But you need not cower. He's not trying to exclude you. Rather, He invites you to come. He *delights* to have you come!

But there's still more here. We don't come to the Father through Jesus only on the day of our conversion. We won't gain access to the Father only on the day of our deaths. Rather, Jesus gives us access into God's presence *every time we pray*. We pray in Jesus' name, claiming the Son's unique prerogatives (John 14:13–14; 15:26; 16:23–24). We enter into God's presence through the new and living way that Jesus opened by His sacrifice (Hebrews 10:19–20). We come to the Father—day after day after day—through Jesus.

Yes, there would be a parting when Jesus returned to the Father. We feel His absence acutely, two millennia later. But it is temporary.

Our very real sorrow will ultimately yield to unspeakable, unshakeable joy:

> So also you have sorrow now, but I will see you again, and your hearts will rejoice, and no one will take your joy from you. (John 16:22)

I am with you, says the Savior,
Even to the age's end.
Never leaving, nor forsaking,
I'm your ever-present Friend.
Fear not, loved one; hear My comfort:
None can pluck you from My hand.
Trust me, loved one; I am constant:
None can change what I have planned.

Come be with Me, says the Master,
Greeting hopeful, homesick eyes.
I was with you in your journey;
Be with Me in paradise.
Fear not, loved one; know My promise:
I will surely, quickly come.
Trust me, loved one; know My purpose:
I will bring you safely home.[16]

∼

---

[16] Chris Anderson and Greg Habegger, "I Am with You" (Church Works Media, 2013).

DAY 5

JESUS' PROMISE OF THE HOLY SPIRIT
John 14, 15, 16

Jesus was departing. The disciples were despondent.

But Jesus had a parting Gift for them, and for every true believer ever since. Jesus' final night of teaching was punctuated with promises that He would send to them the Holy Spirit. It's a stupendous promise. And it had a remarkable fulfilment.

Jesus' sending of the Spirit merits a book, not a few pages in a devotional. But let's attempt to glimpse the significance of the Spirit's coming. Of course, the Spirit had been active throughout the Old Testament. And He was active in Jesus' ministry. But something new was coming. Something unprecedented. In the upper room, Jesus emphasized two main themes regarding the Spirit's coming: The Holy Spirit would replace the Lord Jesus, and the Holy Spirit would help and comfort the disciples.

The Spirit would be the Vicar of Christ.

As we noted on Day 4, Jesus repeatedly predicted His approaching departure, both temporarily in His death and subsequently in His return to the Father. But, in deep empathy and compassion, He followed up this hard news with a new hope: He would not leave His children as orphans (John 14:8), though that is precisely how they felt on first hearing of Jesus' looming exit. Abandoned. Frightened. Vulnerable, like children who had lost their parents. And yet, when He left, Jesus explained, He and the Father would send the Holy Spirit. He emphasized this world-changing promise again and again and again:

> I will ask the Father, and he will give you another Helper, to be with you forever, even the Spirit of truth, whom the world

cannot receive, because it neither sees him nor knows him. You know him, for he dwells with you and will be in you.... But the Helper, the Holy Spirit, whom the Father will send in my name, he will teach you all things and bring to your remembrance all that I have said to you. (John 14:16–17, 26)

But when the Helper comes, whom I will send to you from the Father, the Spirit of truth, who proceeds from the Father, he will bear witness about me. (John 15:26)

When the Spirit of truth comes, he will guide you into all the truth, for he will not speak on his own authority, but whatever he hears he will speak, and he will declare to you the things that are to come. He will glorify me, for he will take what is mine and declare it to you. (John 16:13–14)

It is especially noteworthy that the Spirit would replace Jesus Himself, post-Pentecost. He would be the Vicar of Christ—Jesus' replacement and stand-in. No human, in Rome or elsewhere, has the prerogative to claim such a title. But the Spirit is coequal with the Father and the Son—so much so that the Spirit's presence is essentially Jesus' presence. So Jesus can promise never to leave or forsake us (Matthew 28:20; Hebrews 13:5), and can *fulfill* that promise through the presence of the Holy Spirit.

R. A. Torrey writes,

> Now that Jesus is gone to the Father, we have another person, just as divine as He is, just as wise as He, just as strong as He, just as loving as He, just as tender as He, just as ready, and just as able to help, who is always right by our side.[17]

My only amendment would be that whereas Jesus was "right by our side," the Spirit is actually *inside* us. Which brings us to the next point of Jesus' teaching regarding the Spirit.

The Spirit would be the Helper of Christians.

We might be tempted to think of the Spirit as a mere consolation prize, a second-rate substitute for the real article. But we would

---

[17] R. A. Torrey, *The Person and Work of the Holy Spirit* (New Kensington, PA: Whitaker House, 1996), 74–75.

be entirely mistaken. Jesus promised, straight-faced, that the Spirit's presence on Earth would be *more advantageous* than His very own presence:

> Nevertheless, I tell you the truth: *it is to your advantage that I go away*, for if I do not go away, the Helper will not come to you. But if I go, I will send him to you. (John 16:7)

The disciples' interaction with the divine would actually be *upgraded* under the Spirit's ministry. Is that modesty on the part of Jesus? Hyperbole? Or is it reality?

Though it is an audacious claim, it is reality. Jesus' followers are better served by His absence than by His presence in this era. Which means we severely undervalue the Spirit's ministry to us! John Owen comments on the Spirit's significance with his typical profundity:

> When God designed the great and glorious work of recovering fallen man in the saving of sinners, to the praise of the glory of his grace, he appointed, in his infinite wisdom, two great means thereof. The one was *the giving of his Son for them*, and the other was *the giving of his Spirit unto them*. And hereby was way made for the manifestation of the glory of the whole blessed Trinity; which is the utmost end of all the works of God.[18]

In what sense is the Spirit's presence an improvement? First, during His incarnation, Jesus' physical presence was in one place at a time—a manger, a dusty road, a synagogue. G. Campbell Morgan writes that Christ was "limited and localized, and men had to wait for an opportunity to converse."[19] But the Spirit has no such limitations. He is in every believer, in every place, without spatial boundaries.

Moreover, the Holy Spirit is the Member of the Trinity Who most intimately interacts with Christians in this era. We interact directly with the Spirit—not the Father or the Son. This point cannot be overemphasized, especially to conservative Christians who are prone

---

18   John Owen, *The Works of John Owen*, Volume 3, ed. William H. Goold (Carlisle, PA: The Banner of Truth Trust, 1965), 23.

19   G. Campbell Morgan, "The Results of the Spirit's Coming" in *Understanding the Holy Spirit* ed. G. Campbell Morgan and Charles H. Spurgeon (Chattanooga, TN: AMG Publishers, 1995), 81.

to deemphasize the Spirit's ministry in response to perceived overemphases by others.

It is the indwelling *Spirit* Who inspired the Scriptures and now helps us to understand and apply them (John 14:26; 15:26; 16:13–14; 2 Peter 1:21). It is the *Spirit* Who convicts us and opens our eyes to the saving truths of the Bible (John 16:8; 1 Corinthians 2:14). It is the *Spirit* Who gives us spiritual life (John 3:3–8; Titus 3:5). It is the *Spirit* Who seals and keeps us (Ephesians 4:30). It is the *Spirit* Who baptizes us into Christ and His body (Romans 6; 1 Corinthians 12:13). It is the *Spirit* Who helps us fight our sin (Romans 8:13; Galatians 5:16–23). It is the *Spirit* Who gives us assurance of our salvation (Romans 8:15–16). It is the *Spirit* Who assists us in prayer (Romans 8:26–27). It is the *Spirit* Who progressively changes us into Christlikeness (2 Corinthians 3:18). It is the *Spirit* Who gifts us for service to the body of Christ (1 Corinthians 12:4–11).

I ask, then—have we not undervalued Him and His ministry?

The Christian's life is granted by the power of the Spirit, is sustained by the power of the Spirit, and is impossible apart from the power of the Spirit. Jesus, in His great mercy, has sent us a Helper ... a Comforter ... a *Paraklete*—One Who comes alongside us to help. Just as Jesus is our Advocate in heaven (1 John 2:1–2), so the Spirit is our Advocate on Earth.

And once that promised, blessed Spirit arrived at Pentecost, the disciples—and indeed the world—would never be the same.

> *Blessed Spirit, meet our need;*
> *In our silence intercede.*
> *Translate groans we cannot speak,*
> *Heal the broken, help the weak.*[20]

---

[20] Chris Anderson and Molly Ijames "A Triune Prayer" (Beckenhorst Press, 2010).

DAY 6

JESUS, THE LIFE-GIVING VINE
John 15:1–11

John's Gospel contains seven great "I am" statements from the Lord Jesus. In John 15 we arrive at the one that is perhaps most difficult to understand: "I am the true vine" (vv. 1, 4).

The allegory is rich, and Jesus Himself explains its meaning. He is the Vine.[21] The Father is the Vinedresser—the "farmer" (v. 1). We disciples are branches. Those who are vitally connected to Jesus bring forth fruit (vv. 2, 4, 5, 8). Those who are not, who merely have the *appearance* of connection, will be cut off and burned (v. 6). Though there is debate about who those fruitless, fraudulent vines may be, in context it's Judas. Don't be like him!

Throughout the upper-room discourse, Jesus often returns to several primary lessons. We can trace those motifs in John 15. I'm going to suggest three.

Jesus commands us to obey.

Jesus' teaching is remarkably gracious. But we make a mistake if we miss His repeated calls to keep His commandments. I confess that at times I have so emphasized the doctrine of justification—the glorious truth that we are clothed in Jesus' righteousness—that I have deemphasized Scripture's commands for us to fight our sin, obey biblical commands, and pursue practical holiness. In the mouth of Jesus, practical holiness generally comes down to one pregnant word: *obedience.*

Perhaps you are acquainted with teaching on "love languages." The concept is that each of us are hardwired to prioritize one of five ways

---

21 Although it is beyond the scope of this study, the imagery of Jesus as the Vine has its roots in the Old Testament. Jesus presents Himself as the fulfilment of those texts, the perfect Israel. See Carson, *Gospel According to John*, 513–14.

of expressing and receiving love: words of affirmation, quality time, acts of service, gifts, or physical touch. They aren't biblical categories, of course, but it's an interesting observation.

Well, Jesus' love language is *obedience*. Again and again, He insists that love for Him is expressed by keeping His commandments. Commitment to Christ is demonstrated not by sincere words or grand gestures, but by obeying His commands:

> If you love me, you will keep my commandments. (John 14:15)
>
> Whoever has my commandments and keeps them, he it is who loves me. (John 14:21)
>
> If you keep my commandments, you will abide in my love, just as I have kept my Father's commandments and abide in his love. (John 15:10)
>
> You are my friends if you do what I command you. (John 15:14)

This is so important that the apostle John, who recorded this teaching from the upper room, makes obeying Christ's commands one of the distinguishing characteristics of a genuine believer in the book of 1 John (1:7; 2:3–6; 3:3, 6–10, 24; 5:2–3, 18).

But there's more. There *must* be more, or we have no hope. Only through Jesus and the indwelling Holy Spirit *can* we do what we *ought* to do. That brings me to the second motif in John 15.

Jesus enables us to obey.
Lest we assume that the obedience which Jesus requires rests on *us*—our effort, our discipline, our grit—Jesus unmistakably emphasizes our ongoing and utter dependence on Him. If one phrase can adequately summarize Jesus' teaching in John 15 it would be this: "Apart from me you can do nothing" (John 15:5b).

The hope of Christian vitality rests not on our hard work or sincerity, but on our connection to Jesus, the life-giving, sap-supplying *Vine*. "Christ dwells principally on this," John Calvin tells us, "that the vital sap—that is, all life and strength—proceeds from him alone."[22]

---

22   John Calvin, *Calvin's Commentaries*, trans. William Pringle (Grand Rapids: Baker Books, 1999), 17:107.

Jesus is everything to us! He is the only Source of Christian *life*. He is the only Source of Christian *joy*. And He is the only Source of Christian *fruit*. That's another major focus of John 15—that life is evidenced by fruit (vv. 2, 4, 5, 8, 16). The fruit we are after varies in its forms, from new disciples (John 4:36) to Christians virtues (Galatians 5:22–23). But Christians *will* produce fruit, thereby bringing glory to God (John 15:8).

Now, it's tempting to teach John 15 in a merely transactional or utilitarian way. Candidly, in the first draft of this chapter I did so: *You must obey, and Jesus enables you to obey. So get busy producing fruit ... and good luck!*

But Jesus isn't trying to stress you out with fruit quotas. That's certainly not the genius of John 15. There is so much more here.

Most importantly, Jesus brings us into vital communion with Himself.

More than anything, John 15 is about fellowship with Christ. With almost comical redundancy, Jesus commands us to *abide* (John 15:4, 5, 6, 7, 9, 10)—in *Him*, in *His Word*, and in *His love*. The key to this passage—and the key to Christian living—is sweet, fulfilling, joy-inducing intimacy with Jesus. Every Christian has spiritual union with Christ. William Hendriksen describes our union with Jesus as "moral, mystical, and spiritual" before concluding that "it is a union founded on love."[23]

Exactly so. Of course the Christian experience includes commands, fruit production, and some painful but profitable pruning. But Christianity isn't *about* those things. It's about Jesus. Our Lord makes it abundantly clear that He desires our good. Just listen to the climax of this portion of His teaching!

> These things I have spoken to you that my joy may be in you, and that your joy may be full. (John 15:11)

We're not being used. Rather, we are being nurtured and nourished. The healthy Christian life has more in common with a greenhouse

---

[23] William Hendriksen, *New Testament Commentary: Exposition of the Gospel According to John* (Grand Rapids, MI: Baker Academic, 1953), 2:297.

than a factory.[24] Yes, communion with Jesus results in fruit. But even more so, it results in joy. How can it not? The greatest blessing of our connection to Christ—is *Christ!* We don't just get productivity, or reward, or even heaven. We get *Him*!

I can't do better than John Piper on this important point:

> God is the gospel. That is, he is what makes the good news good. Nothing less can make the gospel good news. God is the final and highest gift that makes the good news good. Until people use the gospel to get to God, they use it wrongly.[25]

> *We are saved by grace alone—*
> *Undeserved, yet freely shown;*
> *No accomplishment on earth*
> *Can achieve the second birth.*

> *We will stand on Christ alone,*
> *The unyielding Cornerstone;*
> *Nations rage and devils roar,*
> *Still He reigns forevermore!*

> *Glory be, glory be to God alone*
> *Through the church He redeemed and made His own.*
> *He has freed us, He will keep us till we're safely home;*
> *Glory be, glory be to God alone!*[26]

---

24 I am grateful to Pastor Cary Schmidt for this insightful analogy.

25 John Piper, *God Is the Gospel: Meditations on God's Love as the Gift of Himself* (Wheaton, IL: Crossway Books, 2005), 42.

26 Chris Anderson and Bob Kauflin, "Reformation Hymn" (Sovereign Grace Music and Church Works Media, 2017).

DAY 7

JESUS' DISCIPLES AND THE HOSTILE WORLD
John 15:18–25

Our God is the "God of all comfort" (2 Corinthians 1:3). During the upper-room discourse, Jesus repeatedly promised to send the Holy Spirit, the One the King James Version describes as "the Comforter" (John 14:16, 26; 15:26; 16:7). We are not alone. But Jesus never withholds from His disciples difficult truths. He is too good, too compassionate, too honest to hide from us the challenges of following Him.

And so, the upper-room discourse also includes the full disclosure that following Jesus will put us at enmity with the world. Specifically, the world will hate us if we love Jesus. Believers reading this in the twenty-first century may have a theoretical understanding of this. But Jesus' disciples were hours away from Jesus' arrest and murder, and they would finish the night running for their lives as "the world" invaded the Garden of Gethsemane. Though they escaped on that particular night, ten of the eleven disciples would die martyrs' deaths. Try to feel the weight of Jesus' words in that historical context.

The world which hated the Lord Jesus will hate His servants.

Jesus' teaching on persecution in the upper room is a reprise of a message He had preached at the very commencement of His ministry. In the Sermon on the Mount, Jesus included a blessing on those who suffer for His sake:

> Blessed are those who are persecuted for righteousness' sake, for theirs is the kingdom of heaven. Blessed are you when others revile you and persecute you and utter all kinds of evil against you falsely on my account. Rejoice and be glad, for your reward

is great in heaven, for so they persecuted the prophets who were before you. (Matthew 5:10–12)

The fact that the world will hate Christians formed a major motif of Jesus' teaching throughout His time on earth (Matthew 10:22–25; 16:24; 24:9; John 15:18, 19, 23, 24, 25; 17:14). Our surprise—our utter indignation!—when the world opposes Christianity in our lifetime shows how little we've heeded our Savior's warnings.

Jesus, just hours from His own martyrdom, reminds the disciples that the world will never be a true friend of Christ or Christians. But we are in good company. The world hates Jesus (John 15:18). It hates the Father (John 15:23–24). And it will hate us if we are faithful (John 15:18–19).

The reason the world so opposes believers is that we are different. We have been called by Jesus *"out of the world"* (John 15:19), thereby earning the hatred of the world. As John 17 will make clear, we are not called out of the world in a physical sense. Jesus has left us *in* the world to exert influence *on* the world, though we are not *of* the world (John 17:11, 14–16). But we have come out of the world in a *spiritual* sense. When we are born again, our character changes. Our conduct changes. Our values change. Our loyalties change. And as a result, the world resents us. If they don't, perhaps we should do some soul-searching to determine why.

While the apostles initially seemed to chafe at this teaching, they eventually understood it. Peter counsels us not to think of persecution as "strange," but as an honor (1 Peter 4:12–19). John tells us not to be surprised when the world hates us (1 John 3:13). And Paul informs us that "all who desire to live a godly life in Christ Jesus will be persecuted" (2 Timothy 3:12). It's not in the fine print of Scripture. It's printed in bold, underlined, and italicized: Pleasing Jesus will displease the world.

The true gospel is inherently offensive to the unsaved.

There are times, to be sure, when Christians invite the censure of the world by being unreasonably backwards or critical. It is no virtue to be offensive in your demeanor. Although Jesus was sinless, sinners wanted to be near Him. That's our example. For us, as for Christ, the world's hatred should be "without a cause" (John 15:25; Psalm 35:19).

But even for the most winsome of witnesses, the message of the cross is an offense. The doctrine of human depravity offends. The doctrine of the penal atonement offends. The doctrine of the eternality of hell offends. In particular, the doctrine of the exclusivity of the Christian gospel—that there is no salvation apart from faith in Jesus Christ (John 14:6; Acts 4:12)—offends, especially in a world addicted to approval and allergic to absolutes.

Calvin writes, "The Gospel cannot be published without instantly driving the world to rage. Consequently, it will never be possible for godly teachers to avoid the hatred of the world."[27]

Which leads me to my final point.

The antipathy of the world should inspire Christians to love one another.

In light of the world's hatred of Jesus' disciples, we come to understand the importance of His repeated commands to love one another, as discussed on Day 2 of this study. Love for fellow Christians is to be *the* most distinctive characteristic of Jesus' disciples. We should be recognized by the unsaved for our other-worldly love for each other, despite our differences of background, culture, or opinion. First John emphasizes Jesus' new commandment even more urgently, insisting that those who don't love Christians *aren't* Christians (1 John 3:10, 14, 17; 4:8, 20).

Every Christian knows the heartache of "friendly fire"—when Christians turn on one another. The Lord Jesus intends His church to be a refuge for His people, not a battle zone. Satan is the accuser of the brethren. The unsaved are our oppressors. Neither Satan nor the world need the church's "help" roughing up believers.[28]

---

27 John Calvin, *Calvin's Commentaries*, trans. William Pringle (Grand Rapids: Baker Books, 1999), 18:123.

28 For more on this, see my book *The Scandal of Schism: A Journey from Sinful Division to Biblical Fidelity* (Church Works Media, 2024).

My favorite commentator on the Gospels, J. C. Ryle, offers this interpretation of Jesus' words:

> I press on you these repeated charges to love one another, because you must expect the hatred of the world. The more the world hates you, the more you ought to love one another and stick together.[29]

The Scriptures know nothing of Christians who are friends with the world (1 John 2:15; James 4:4). Should we be friends with *sinners*? Absolutely. Our Savior was. We should form redemptive relationships with the lost, praying that the Lord will open their eyes to the truth. We are still *in* the world. But we are not *of* it. We are not *like* it. The culture which is antagonistic to *Him* will be antagonistic to *His*. Expect it, and even rejoice in it for Jesus' sake.

How dark the night that shrouds the world
Where war and anguish reign;
How fierce our swords, how sharp our words,
How piercing is our pain.
O Christ, return like blazing dawn—
The Morning Star of Light!
The Lord Himself will be our Sun
And day eclipse the night.[30]

---

29 J. C. Ryle, *Expository Thoughts on the Gospels: John 10:31–21:25* (Grand Rapids, MI: Baker Book House, 2007), 2:119.

30 Chris Anderson and Greg Habegger, "How Dark the Night" (Church Works Media, 2022).

DAY 8

JESUS' GLORY IN THE CROSS
John 12, 13, and 17

The cross of Christ was a stumbling block to the Jews (1 Corinthians 1:23). And the disciples were Jews, so the cross was a stumbling block to them as well. Jesus' first mention of the cross was met with a rebuke from Peter, the student body president of the disciples (Matthew 16:21–23).

In a sense, we can understand why this was such a hard pill to swallow. For a sweaty, dusty, thirty-year-old man to claim to be the Son of God was an assertion which, by itself, required an almost painful stretch for orthodox Jews. It felt idolatrous to recognize a "man" as a deity. One of the primary lessons of their entire Old Testament history was that God judges idolatry. And they got it. We read of no overt idolatry after the Babylonian captivity. So, recognizing Jesus as God's Son was difficult—though for those who humbly studied the Old Testament Scriptures, there were scores of predictions.

Of course, Jesus' countless miracles bore further testimony to His deity, as did His unprecedented teaching. I'm not excusing the Jews' disbelief. But the idea of Jehovah taking on human flesh was a lot to take in. And the idea of Jehovah *dying*, especially via the scandal of *crucifixion*—that was almost too much for even the strongest believers to absorb.

To us, the cross is a sign of hope. We place elegant crosses around our necks. They adorn our church buildings. They are included as décor in weddings, the most joyful of occasions. They stir in us feelings of gratitude and devotion.

Because the cross is celebrated in Christian culture, we almost forget that crucifixion was the most inglorious of deaths—not only painful but shameful. It was the death of notorious criminals. Roman citizens, regardless of how heinous their crimes, could not be crucified. It was too low, too vile, too humiliating. The cross was a scandal. It called forth feelings of revulsion, not reverence. There's a reason why Philippians 2:8 climaxes Jesus' voluntary humiliation with almost awestruck words: "he humbled himself by becoming obedient to the point of death, *even death on a cross.*"

MacArthur writes,

> Aside from the physical pain of crucifixion, the most notable feature of this type of execution was the stigma of disgrace that was attached to it. Victims were mercilessly taunted. They were usually hanged naked. They were deliberately made a spectacle of shame and reproach. Hebrews 12:2 refers to this when it says Christ "endured the cross, despising the shame."[31]

And yet, the Lord Jesus repeatedly insisted that it was the cross by which He would climactically *glorify* the Father (John 13:31). That message is especially clear in John 12:27–28, where Jesus' submission to the coming cross earned an audible answer from His Father:

> "Now is my soul troubled. And what shall I say? 'Father, save me from this hour'? But for this purpose I have come to this hour. Father, glorify your name." Then a voice came from heaven: "I have glorified it, and I will glorify it again."

The hour Jesus spoke of was the approach of His crucifixion. And yet, that hour would bring *glory* to the Father—not shame, as everyone but the Godhead assumed. We see the same truth repeated in John 17:1: "When Jesus had spoken these words, he lifted up his eyes to heaven, and said, 'Father, the hour has come; glorify your Son that the Son may glorify you.'"

Jesus transformed the cross—a gruesome object of ancient torture—into a symbol of divine triumph. The cross glorifies Jesus, for it

---

31 John MacArthur, *The Murder of Jesus: A Study of How Jesus Died* (Nashville, TN: Word Publishing, 2000), 202.

demonstrates more than anything else in the world the depth of His love. It glorifies the Father, for it shows the wisdom of His plan and the beautiful, willing submission of the Son.

Thus, the cross has become a cause for celebration and glory for believers as well. It is our *only* source of glory, in fact. We boast, Paul writes in Galatians 6:14—we *glory*, the KJV says—in the cross of Christ. I love how the hymn-writer so aptly put it:

> My sinful self my only shame,
> My glory all the cross.[32]

Look again at John 12:27–28 and John 17:1. Jesus prayed that the Father would glorify Him *through* the cross, not by a miraculous deliverance from it. God answered that prayer. The Father did glorify the Son. The Father was glorified by the Son. And Jesus continued His relentless march to Calvary.

> *Can this be God—this Baby wrapped in swaddling clothes?*
> *Can this be God—the ageless One, now moments old?*
> *The unseen God—now manifest in human form?*
> *Yes, this is God; Immanuel at last is born.*
>
> *Can this be God—this sweaty, thirsty, homeless Man?*
> *Can this be God—with weary feet and calloused hands?*
> *Almighty God—fatigued beneath His blazing sun?*
> *Yes, this is God, and this is Man, now merged in One.*
>
> *Can this be God—this bloody mass pinned to a tree?*
> *Can this be God—this spectacle between two thieves?*
> *The Most High God—with tears of anguish on His face?*
> *Yes, this is God, Who suffers in the sinner's place.*

---

32 Elizabeth Cecilia Clephane, "Beneath the Cross of Jesus." Public domain.

Can this be God—this lifeless corpse inside a tomb?
Can this be God—His glory turned to lightless gloom?
Immortal God—Who somehow breathed His final breath?
Yes, this is God, Who ransomed sinners by His death.

Yes, this is God—this Victor Who escaped the grave.
And this is God—this risen Lamb with pow'r to save.
Triumphant God—Who shall forever be adored;
Yes, this is God, the King of kings and Lord of lords.[33]

~

---

33 Chris Anderson, "Can This Be God?" (Church Works Media, 2025).

DAY

JESUS, THE NEW PASSOVER
Matthew 26:17–30

The Passover was instituted by God as a memorial of His mighty deliverance of Israel from their bondage in Egypt (Exodus 12:21–28). By the time Jesus gathered with His disciples in the upper room, the Jews had observed the rite for almost 1,500 years.

We tend to romanticize the sacrifice of Passover lambs. I've seen children's books which show a cuddly lamb, perhaps with a trickle of blood coming from its neck. I understand that. There's no need to give children needless nightmares. But make no mistake, the Passover was a bloody event.

All Israel gathered in Jerusalem. A sacrificial lamb was slain for every Jewish family, meaning that there were tens of thousands of sacrifices taking place on the Temple mount. R. Kent Hughes estimates that "more than two hundred thousand lambs were slain."[34] The Law called for the blood of the sacrifices to be splashed against the altar (Exodus 24:6; 29:12, 16, 20), and the fat and entrails of the lamb were burned on the altar. I can almost smell the carcasses, the blood, and the billowing smoke. Yes, it reminded the Jews of God's deliverance. But it also reminded them of His wrath.

As a faithful Jew, Jesus would have observed the Passover more than thirty times in His lifetime. However, the observance on the night He spent in the upper room with His closest friends would be different. In one sense it would be the last Jewish Passover, at least from a Christian perspective. As sacred as the traditional Passover was, Jesus superseded it. In the upper room, He presented Himself as the fulfillment and replacement of the Passover.

---

34 R. Kent Hughes, "Gethsemane" in *Jesus, Keep Me Near the Cross: Experiencing the Passion and Power of Easter*, ed. Nancy Guthrie (Wheaton, IL: Crossway Books, 2009), 32.

Jesus is the ultimate Passover Lamb.

The connections between Jesus' death and the Passover lambs could not be clearer. He died at the same *time* as the Passover lambs (compare Matthew 26:2 with Luke 22:15). He died in the same *place* as the Passover lambs. He died for the same *purpose* as the Passover lambs, although in an infinitely greater way.

Just as the Passover celebrated what we might call "deliverance by death," Jesus emphasized the saving consequence of His own approaching death. We can become so familiar with Jesus' words on this night that they no longer shock us. But again and again, Jesus spoke with remarkable focus and almost unnerving calm of His Own death:

> This is my body, which is given for you. (Luke 22:19)

> This is my blood of the covenant, which is poured out for many for the forgiveness of sins. (Matthew 26:28)

> Do this in remembrance of me. (Luke 22:19; 1 Corinthians 11:24–25)

In their book *Pierced for Our Transgressions*, Steve Jeffery, Michael Ovey, and Andrew Sach explain that Jesus broke from the Passover script by relating the wine and bread to Himself, not the paschal lamb. They write,

> Jesus' references to his "body," and in particular his "blood ... poured out," allude to his death, which he thus sets forth as the decisive fulfilment of the Passover festival. Whereas the old Passover focused on the body and blood of a lamb, slain as a penal substitutionary sacrifice for the redemption of Israel, the Lord's Supper focuses on the body and blood of Christ, who gave himself as a penal substitutionary sacrifice for his people.[35]

Most significantly, Jesus bore God's wrath in a way prophesied by the first Passover lambs. He died as a substitute, experiencing death

---

35 Steve Jeffery, Michael Ovey, and Andrew Sach, *Pierced for Our Transgressions: Rediscovering the Glory of Penal Substitution* (Wheaton, IL: Crossway Books, 2007), 39.

in our place, that we might be spared. Spared from what? *From God.* If we miss this, we misunderstand both the Passover event and the new and perfect paschal Lamb. Israel's deliverance on that final night in Egypt wasn't just from Egypt. It was from God.

During the first Passover, God's wrath was poured out on the sacrificial lamb so that it wouldn't touch God's people. According to Hebrews 11:28, Moses "kept the Passover and sprinkled the blood, so that the Destroyer of the firstborn might not touch them." On that evening, the people of Israel were delivered from "the Destroyer"—from the angel of the Lord who would see the blood of the lamb and "pass over" those for whom it was shed (Exodus 12:12–13, 23).

In the same way, Jesus absorbed God's wrath in our place. God the Father looks on the blood of the Lamb of God so that His wrath might *pass over* us! Paul makes this connection clear: "Christ, our Passover lamb, has been sacrificed" (1 Corinthians 5:7). Jesus shed His blood to redeem us—not from bondage in Egypt, but from a greater bondage to sin. And He delivered us from God.

Jesus instituted the ultimate Passover feast.

Just as Jesus replaced the Passover lamb, He also replaced the Passover feast when He instituted the Lord's Table. Just as the Israelites were to remember the one-time Passover deliverance by perpetual Passover observances, Christians are now called to remember the one-time redeeming sacrifice of Christ by eating reminders of His broken body and shed blood. "In remembrance of me" were His words as He established this new ordinance (Luke 22:19).

For the first two decades of my Christian life, I kind of missed the point of the Lord's Table. While we are exhorted to examine ourselves (1 Corinthians 11:28), our primary focus should be on Jesus. For too long I partook of the Lord's Table in remembrance of *me*—my sins, my confession, my earnestness. But Jesus gave us the new Passover meal so that we would remember *Him*—"the Lamb of God, who takes away the sin of the world" (John 1:29).

The Lord's Table is a remembrance of Jesus' death. But it is also a reminder of sweet fellowship. The original Passover meal was a festive time, not a mournful one. It was, if you will, a *holiday meal*—one that included the roasted Passover lamb, bitter herbs, and unleavened bread, as well as a joyful retelling of the history of Israel especially suited to young children.[36] Just so, the Lord's Table need not be morose but should include an element of celebration, hope, and intimacy with our Savior. As the ultimate paschal Lamb, Jesus doesn't only deliver us—He *nourishes* us. He welcomes us. He gives us a seat at the Father's table. A. B. Bruce writes,

> As often as the Lord's Supper is celebrated we are invited to contemplate Christ as the food of our souls.... As often as we eat the bread and drink the cup we declare that Christ has been, and is now, our soul's food in all these ways. And as often as we use this Supper with sincerity we are helped to appropriate Christ as our spiritual food more and more abundantly.[37]

> *Behold the Lamb, the dying Lamb,*
> *Who takes away just wrath.*
> *God saw the blood of His Beloved*
> *And over us has passed.*

> *Gaze on the Christ, our Sacrifice,*
> *On altar made of wood.*
> *Worship the Lamb, the worthy Lamb,*
> *Who bought us with His blood.*[38]

---

36 Alfred Edersheim, *Sketches of Jewish Social Life in the Days of Christ* (Grand Rapids, MI: William B. Eerdmans Publishing Company, 1978), 110.

37 A. B. Bruce, *The Training of the Twelve* (Grand Rapids, MI: Kregel Publications: 1988), 365.

38 Chris Anderson and Greg Habegger, "Gaze on the Christ" (Church Works Media, 2011).

D A Y

JESUS' FRAIL FRIENDS
Luke 22:14–30

The ministry of Jesus is filled with miracles. Perhaps the greatest miracle of all is that He eventually used His selfish, sleepy, sophomoric disciples to turn the world upside down (Acts 17:6). Only a master general could conquer the world with such a motley band of soldiers. It's remarkable.

The disciples were geniuses at *missing the point*. Perhaps it was stupidity. More likely, it was stubbornness. But whenever Jesus spoke of His approaching agonies, the disciples either rebuked Him, ignored Him, or changed the subject (Luke 9:44–46; 18:31–34). And of all times, it happened—again—in the upper room. Only Luke shares this particular event, highlighting the disciples' folly as a foil to Jesus' remarkable grace. "It is sad," Leon Morris writes, "that, with Jesus so close to the cross, His most intimate disciples were so far from His spirit."[39]

The disciples responded to Jesus' suffering with crass ambition.
Jesus had just finished instituting the Lord's Table. It was an historic moment, and likely an emotional time since it was so closely connected to His death. And yet, the disciples' immediate response to His teaching was to renew their argument over who among them would be the greatest. They greeted the New Covenant with irreverent rivalry.

Perhaps it was Jesus' prophecy that one of them would betray Him that led the disciples to argue (Luke 22:21–22). Instead of rallying to Him when He shared this grievous news, they bickered at one another. Their initial moments of self-doubt (Luke 22:23) quickly gave way to self-confidence (Luke 22:24).

---

39 Leon Morris, *The Gospel According to St. Luke: An Introduction and Commentary* (Grand Rapids, MI: William B. Eerdmans Publishing Company, 1974), 307.

A. B. Bruce provides another explanation for their rivalry. As Jesus had the disciples partake of the wine of the New Covenant, He told them that He wouldn't partake of the cup again until He did so with them *in His kingdom* (Luke 22:18). The only word they heard, apparently, was *kingdom*. Bruce writes, "The allusion to the kingdom was quite sufficient to set their imaginations on fire and re-awaken old dreams about thrones, and from old dreams to old feuds and jealousies the transition was natural and easy."[40]

Jesus responded to the disciples' frailty with grace.
Again, this wasn't the first fight over preeminence (Luke 9:46; Mark 10:35–45). The Lord Jesus must have felt like a babysitter at times. We would excuse Him had He slapped the table, berated the disciples, or even fired them all and started over. The Lord "knows our frame" and "remembers that we are dust," Psalm 103:14 says. And mercy, the disciples were *dusty*.

And yet, Jesus was a model of patience.

First, He instructed them—again—that to fight for first place is worldly, the way kings of the Gentiles act (Luke 22:25). He reminded them that His kingdom is different and that the greatest would be those who serve (Luke 22:26). He had shown them that very night that even though He was the Most High God, He had come to serve (Luke 22:27; John 13:3–5). Admittedly, that lesson hadn't exactly taken. Not yet. But He didn't give up.

Jesus called them to humility and service, and He showed them what it looked like by washing their feet. As my friend Ken Collier says about Christian ministry, "The one who dies with the dirtiest towel wins!"

But Jesus didn't end with this gentle rebuke. He continued, astonishingly, with another word of affirmation. It's a staggering statement given its timing. They had been oblivious to Jesus' needs and obsessed with their own. Yet, He commended them:

---

40 Bruce, 343.

DAY 10 — JESUS' FRAIL FRIENDS

You are those who have stayed with me in my trials, and I assign to you, as my Father assigned to me, a kingdom, that you may eat and drink at my table in my kingdom and sit on thrones judging the twelve tribes of Israel. (Luke 22:28–30)

That's grace. Jesus interrupted their argument over who would be the greatest in His kingdom by assuring them that *all of them* would. He looked past their weakness, even in that moment. He thanked them for staying with Him through His trials—knowing full well that they would forsake Him during His greatest trial, just a few hours later. He told them that just as they ate and drank with Him in the relatively humble upper room, they would eat and drink with Him again in His kingdom. Indeed, they would be enthroned and would judge God's chosen people!

What a gentle Savior we serve. How marvelously gracious He is. How compassionate, and uplifting, and optimistic, and patient, and empowering. How very, very *good*.

I love this passage because I'm one of Jesus' frail friends. I'm dusty. I fail, miserably, more often than I care to remember. I'd not put up with me.

But Jesus does. And just as He transformed His frail friends into champions who would live—and even die—for His name's sake, He continues His sanctifying work in us. In spite of us. For His glory.

Grace.

To hearts that sink in shame
When sin again has stirred,
To those who drown in blame
The gospel has a word:
"Grace to you. Grace to you."

To all who long to grow,
But hate the things they do,
To those whose hope is low,
The Savior speaks to you:
"Grace to you. Grace to you."

Grace that seeks, grace that keeps,
Grace sufficient to sustain the one who weeps,
Grace to break your sin's embrace,
God's relentless, boundless, endless amazing grace. [41]

---

41   Chris Anderson and Heather Schopf, "Grace to You" (Forever Be Sure, 2024).

DAY 11

JESUS' HIGH-PRIESTLY PRAYER
John 17

The Gospels regularly draw our attention to the prayer life of the Lord Jesus. He was often up early in the morning or going off alone overnight to find time to pray. We might expect, then, that much of His final twenty-four hours would be spent in prayerful preparation for His tremendous trial. And we would be right.

The Gospels record two intense times of prayer for our Lord on this last night, the first in the upper room and the second in Gethsemane. The two seasons of prayer were likely separated by a mere ten-minute walk. But they couldn't have been more distinct from each other.

The first prayer time we often call "Jesus' high-priestly prayer." It reads like a continuation of the teaching in John 13 through 16, or better, the culmination of it. In it, Jesus enjoyed sweet fellowship with the Father and prayed for the protection and unity of His disciples. But the second prayer time was *dark*. It focused exclusively on Jesus' approaching sacrifice. We'll consider it on Day 12.

John 17 feels like the Alps of the entire book of John, an absolutely breathtaking portion of Scripture. I'll apologize now for the inadequacy of this summary. That said, we'll take note of three movements in Jesus' prayer: He prayed for Himself (17:1–5), for His disciples (17:6–19), and finally for His disciples-to-come—for us (17:20–26).

Jesus prayed about His own love and unity with the Father.

Jesus' focus on His own relationship with the Father was relatively brief, covering only John 17:1–5, though the theme resurfaces during His intercession for the disciples. He began His prayer by anticipating His return to the Father and to the glory He relinquished by coming to earth (17:1, 5). He clearly delighted in the intimacy He shared with the Father—an intimacy He longed to see shared with His disciples.

The opening phrase of the prayer, "the hour has come," points to the agonies that awaited Jesus on the cross (17:1). But He didn't yet dread the approaching night. Rather, He looked past the "sufferings" and anticipated the "subsequent glories" (1 Peter 1:11)—the mutual glorification of both the Father and the Son through what would otherwise seem the most inglorious of events: the crucifixion.

John 17:3 provides a lovely encapsulation of the gospel: "This is eternal life, that they know you, the only true God, and Jesus Christ whom you have sent." Knowing God through Christ is not merely the *means* by which we are saved—it is the *prize*. Eternal life *is knowing God!* Many believers miss this point. I did in my early years as a Christian. Through salvation, we aren't only justified; we are *reconciled* to God. We don't just get pardon, or heaven; we get to *know Him, forever!*

John 17:4 follows that encapsulation of gospel privilege with a satisfied, even anticipatory statement from Jesus: "I glorified you on earth, having accomplished the work that you gave me to do." Jesus came to earth to save sinners. But He came, no less, to please the Father.

Jesus prayed for the protection and perseverance of His disciples.

Jesus' prayer for the remaining eleven disciples can be summarized as a prayer for protection and perseverance: "*Keep* them" (17:11, 12, 15). During His ministry, Jesus had won the eleven and kept them, as commissioned by His Father (17:6). Now, in light of His approaching absence, He prayed for the Father to keep them. Leon Morris notes Jesus' almost paternal concern for the eleven:

> He knows that the coming hours will be a great trial to them. Despite everything they are not ready for the shock of Calvary. Tenderly now He commits them to the care of the heavenly Father.[42]

---

42 Leon Morris, *The Gospel According to John* (Grand Rapids, MI: William B. Eerdmans Publishing Company, 1971), 723.

"Keep them," He prays—from *the evil one* (17:15-16), from *sin* (17:17-19), and from *disunity* (17:21).

John 17 provides an essential lesson on Christians' relationship with a hostile world—a world that "has hated them" (17:14). Although we are no longer *of* or *like* the world (17:14, 16), we still remain *in* the world. Indeed, we are *sent into* the world in order to *influence* the world with the gospel (17:15, 18). Jesus' vision for His people was neither monastic isolationism nor pragmatic accommodation. Rather, He left us in the world the way troops are left in occupied territory—we are present, but *on mission*. To use the language of James 1:27, Jesus wants His people to remain unstained by the world ... but also to *stain the world* by exerting gospel influence. Andreas Köstenberger explains:

> Believers, then, are neither to withdraw from the world nor to become indistinguishable from it, but rather, as ones consecrated by the truth and separated from evil, they are to witness to God's Son, aided by the Spirit.[43]

Jesus prayed that the disciples—and disciples yet to come—would share in Trinitarian love.

Jesus' prayer for the eleven transitioned easily into prayer for future saints: "I do not ask for these only, but also for those who will believe in me through their word" (John 17:20). The primary emphasis of Jesus' prayer for the coming ages of Christians, ourselves included, was that we would "all be one" (John 17:21, 22, 23). He certainly wasn't calling for unity at any cost; the entire New Testament warns against complicity with false teachers. But He prayed for a real, vital, gospel-based, Spirit-produced unity—unity so evident in the otherwise diverse body of Christ that even the unbelieving world would notice and marvel at it (John 17:23b).

Köstenberger is helpful once again:

> Jesus' concern for his followers' unity is his greatest burden as his earthly mission draws to a close, and it pervades this entire section. Their unity, in turn, is to be rooted in Jesus' own unity

---

43 Andreas J. Köstenberger, *Baker Exegetical Commentary of the New Testament: John* (Grand Rapids, MI: Baker Academic, 2004), 495.

with the Father. Together with love, unity constitutes a vital prerequisite for their mission.⁴⁴

That is astonishing. Read it again. *Our unity is rooted in Trinitarian unity.* Jesus went on to pray for our inclusion in Trinitarian love. He wants us to be where He is, to share in the glories of heaven (17:24). But there's so much more. He wants us to partake of divine love, which is possible because He has made us partakers of the divine nature (2 Peter 1:4). This is a wondrous, glorious truth: We will spend eternity as partakers—no, *participants*—in the very love which the Father, Son, and Spirit have shared and enjoyed since before time began:

> ... that the love with which you have loved me may be in them, and I in them. (John 17:26)

We are loved. Therefore, we are to love both God and each other. And throughout eternity, we will join in the most powerful force that has ever existed: the love of the Father, Son, and Holy Spirit for One Another. *And now for us!*

> *Relentless love embraced my soul in ages past—*
> *Love undeserved, unknown, yet deep and vast.*
> *God set His love on me—on me, in spite of me!*
> *Salvation's work is His from first to last.*
>
> *Relentless love pursued my heart, though I would hide—*
> *Was unreturned, yet undeterred by pride.*
> *Till by a grace unsought, my rebel soul was caught—*
> *Redeemed by love that would not be denied.*

---

44 Köstenberger, 497.

Relentless love preserves my life from unbelief—
Sustains me through my sin, my doubt, my grief.
Since Christ has done it all, though feeble, I'll not fall,
His wounded hands hold me, the sinners' chief.

Unbounded love, unfailing love,
Love raised upon a tree;
Unending love, prevailing love—
My Savior's sovereign love for me.[45]

~

---

45 Chris Anderson and Greg Habegger, "Relentless Love" (Church Works Media, 2011).

DAY

12

JESUS' AGONY IN THE GARDEN
Matthew 26:31–46

After the Passover feast Jesus and the eleven remaining disciples made their way to one of their favorite retreats, the Garden of Gethsemane. As they walked, Christ foretold that they would all deny Him. Peter led the disciples in protesting and promising fearless fidelity, come what may (Matthew 26:30–35). They would surely remember that bravado, even as they would rue their cowardice.

The walk from the upper room to Gethsemane required around ten minutes. Having crossed the valley of Kidron—little more than a large ravine, really—Jesus and the eleven arrived at the garden, at the base of the Mount of Olives. Our Lord took Peter, James, and John with Him deeper into the garden, where sturdy olive trees cast shadows in the moonlight—trees that remain, sentry-like, two millennia later. What followed was a time of excruciating emotional, mental, and spiritual agony for our Savior. In the garden prayers we gain a glimpse into the very heart of the sinless Son of God. And we learn the astounding cost of our salvation.

There is a well-meaning gospel song that we can sing rather glibly:

> For me it was in the garden he prayed,
> "Not my will, but Thine."
> He shed no tears for his own griefs,
> But sweat drops of blood for mine.[46]

Wrong. Jesus absolutely wept for His own griefs in Gethsemane. Make no mistake: The garden prayer is intended to tether our attention to Jesus' great suffering, not to provide for us a utilitarian self-help lesson on prayer or finding God's will. Though there is much to learn in Gethsemane, *the passage is not about us*. Rather, we

---

46 Charles Hutchinson Gabriel, "My Savior's Love." Public domain.

should gaze with reverent wonder at Christ's unveiled grief in Gethsemane, a foretaste of His grief at Golgotha.

Matthew draws our attention to Jesus' emotional and mental anguish: "He began to be sorrowful and troubled. Then he said to them, 'My soul is very sorrowful, even to death; remain here, and watch with me'" (Matthew 26:37–38). The word *began* gives the impression that these agonies rushed upon the Lord Jesus, suddenly and with deadly force. Remarkably, one of the Savior's burdens was acute loneliness. Alexander Maclaren writes, "Out of the darkness He reaches a hand to feel for the grasp of a friend, and pitifully asks these humble lovers to stay beside Him."[47] "Stay with Me," He said. "Watch with Me." The Almighty looking to His creatures for strength and comfort highlights the infinite mystery of the incarnation (Matthew 26:38, 40).

One would think that on the *one* occasion when our Lord asked for His inner circle's help, they would rally to Him, humbly if not heroically. Instead, unconscionably, they abandoned Him, not in flight but in slumber (Matthew 26:40, 43). His only support would come from a heaven-sent angel who ministered to Him in the stead of His feeble friends (Luke 22:43). Thus, Jesus bore alone the emotional and spiritual trauma that squeezed Him to the breaking point. He fell on His face (Matthew 26:39); He sweat great drops of blood (Luke 22:44); He was vexed to the very brink of death (Matthew 26:38).

This is no hyperbole. Our Master's heart was breaking—so much so that He almost died in the garden. What could cause such shocking agony, such anguish that surprised even Jesus (Mark 14:33)? The answer comes in the words of Christ's pitiful prayer: "Let this cup pass from me" (Matthew 26:39).

The dreaded cup.

What was it? What so filled Christ with horror when He had shown such courageous serenity all through His lifetime? What could make Jesus—the One Who was dauntless before legions of demons and the devil himself—tremble?

---

47   Alexander Maclaren, *The Gospel of St. Matthew* (New York, NY: A. C. Armstrong & Son, 1894), 2: 182.

We must note that Jesus didn't quake in the face of death, as brutal as His death would be. Mere mortals have died courageously all through history, and Jesus Himself had come to Earth for that very purpose. This wasn't cowardice.

No, two deeper agonies tortured the Savior's very soul, each highlighting part of the infinite spiritual suffering that awaited Him at Calvary.

First, Christ dreaded to drink (or experience) the sin of humanity.
The Son, impeccably pure for all eternity, was about to become sin for us (2 Corinthians 5:21). Even the anticipation of such corruption was crushing. Imagine the repulsion our holy, holy, holy Savior felt as He considered being engulfed in the depravity of sinners through the ages! J. C. Ryle writes,

> The real weight that bowed down the heart of Jesus, was the weight of the sin of the world, which seems to have now pressed down upon Him with peculiar force. It was the burden of our guilt imputed to Him, which [would be] laid on Him, as on the head of the scape goat. How great that burden must have been, no heart of man can conceive.[48]

Worse yet, Christ dreaded to experience the wrath of His Father.
Throughout the Scriptures, God's wrath is repeatedly pictured as a cup from which the wicked must drink (Psalm 11:6; Isaiah 51:17, 22; Jeremiah 25:15–16; Revelation 14:10, et al.). Psalm 75:8 is especially clear:

> For in the hand of the Lord there is a cup
> with foaming wine, well mixed,
> and he pours out from it,
> and all the wicked of the earth
> shall drain it down to the dregs.

The Son, Who shared eternal union and fellowship with the Father (John 10:30)—the Beloved, in Whom the Father completely delighted (Matthew 3:17)—would drain the dregs of that cursed

---

48 J. C. Ryle, *Expository Thoughts on the Gospels: Matthew* (Grand Rapids, MI: Baker Book House, 2007), 362.

cup. In the garden that night, He braced Himself to be crushed and forsaken by the Father, all in the place of sinners (Isaiah 53:10). Even the *prospect* of such judgment was overwhelming.

Love for the Father made Jesus dread the cup. And love for the Father also made Him drink it. "Jesus came to the cliff of the cross," Dane Ortlund writes, "and didn't change his mind. He walked over the edge."[49] "Not my will, but Yours be done" (Matthew 26:39, 42).

The Father's will would indeed be done. Jesus would empty the cup (John 18:11), consuming the dregs of God's wrath so that we could be pardoned (1 John 2:2). As John Stott writes, the garden prayer "begins to disclose the enormous costliness of the cross to Jesus."[50]

What grace. What love. And what agony—on a dark night before a darker day.

There was a cup of holy wrath
Which made our fearless Savior quake;
He prayed the cup from Him would pass,
Yet drank its dregs for sinners' sake.

We drink a cup our Lord ordained
To point forgetful hearts above;
With bread it speaks of sinless pain,
Of saving death, of selfless love.[51]

∼

---

49 Dane Ortlund, *Gentle and Lowly: The Heart of Christ for Sinners and Sufferers* (Wheaton, IL: Crossway, 2020), 197.

50 Stott, 75.

51 Chris Anderson and Molly Ijames, "Salvation's Cup" (Church Works Media, 2009).

DAY 13

JESUS' BETRAYAL AND ARREST
Matthew 26:47–56

Having concluded the garden prayer, our Lord took the next step toward the cup He so dreaded. A "great crowd," armed to the teeth as if accosting a dangerous criminal, broke the still night in Gethsemane (Matthew 26:47). Awaking the sleeping disciples, Jesus went out to meet the advancing mob.

The gathering in Gethsemane was a strange one, to be sure. The moonlight, mingled with lanterns and torches (John 18:3), revealed Judas, Jesus' disciple and betrayer. Judas had concealed his wicked heart from his fellow disciples for more than three years. Now, he came to the place he had often frequented with our Lord—a refuge transformed by treason.

Next, we see Temple guards. Though charged with protecting Jehovah's Sanctuary, they came with swords and clubs against Jehovah Himself. We spy the sleepy disciples, led by impetuous Peter. Finally, we see Jesus, the Master, even at His arrest. If there was fear in Gethsemane, it didn't belong to Him. Judas and the throng must have been astonished by Jesus' cool composure.

Judas carried out his treachery in a particularly loathsome way. His intentions were clear enough, but he continued his habitual hypocrisy by betraying Jesus with a kiss (Matthew 26:48–49). Refusing to scorn even Judas, Christ spoke to him as "friend" and urged him to do what he had planned (Matthew 26:50). The statement probably conveys neither sarcasm nor scorn, but pity and grief. It would be the last word Jesus would direct to Judas. David's lament from Psalm 55:12–14 captures the crushing blow of the betrayal:

> For it is not an enemy who taunts me—
> then I could bear it;
> It is not an adversary who deals insolently with me—
> then I could hide from him.
> But it is you, a man, my equal,
> my companion, my familiar friend.
> We used to take sweet counsel together;
> within God's house we walked in the throng.

Peter, momentarily roused from his fear of the mob, lashed out at Malchus, the servant of the High Priest (Matthew 26:51). The clumsy attempt was almost comical. He attacked a servant, not a soldier. Rather than protecting himself and his friends, his assault might have gotten them killed. Most of his fellow disciples were fishermen. None were soldiers. They were obviously no match for their adversaries. Most presumptuously—and characteristically, if we're honest—Peter usurped leadership from the Lord, acting on his own. Again. His folly earned censure from Jesus, not praise (Matthew 26:52–54). Even if his aim had been better and the odds more favorable, his aggression was diametrically opposed to Christ's program. In a statement too many Christians through the centuries have failed to heed, Jesus taught that His cause will not advance by violence (Matthew 26:52).

Jesus' healing of Malchus stirs the imagination (Luke 22:51). It was a final miraculous act of benevolence before His death—another reminder of Jesus' gentleness, a foil for the brutality that awaited Him. It must have given Jesus' captors pause to contrast the power He exerted to help others with the quiet passivity with which He received His own abuse. Even more striking was the contrast between Jesus' kindness and the ferocity of their own religious leaders.

I've often wondered about Malchus' spiritual state after that fateful night. Why is his name even listed when the rest of the throng is anonymous? Could it be that the touch that healed his body eventually brought him to faith? Could it be that we will meet him in heaven?

While the throng's show of force certainly frightened Jesus' disciples, the small army was no match for our Lord. He had the power to annihilate the soldiers, as He proved when He sent them tumbling with a single word (John 18:6). Again, it's a comedic scene to imagine. The closest comparison my mind can summon is the would-be nannies being blown down Cherry Tree Lane just prior to Mary Poppins' arrival at the home of Jane and Michael Banks. Just a word from Jesus—"I Am," significantly—turned an army into so many bowling pins.

Beyond Jesus' own omnipotence, He had at His disposal twelve legions of angels—some 72,000, for those who are counting (Matthew 26:53). Just *one* angel might have managed had He desired deliverance. But He did *not*. He had come to Earth to sacrifice Himself for sinners, and He courageously marched toward the suffering that required. "It must be so," He said (Matthew 26:54). The Scriptures must be fulfilled. The work the Father gave Him to do must be accomplished. The cup that He prayed would pass from Him must be drained: "Shall I not drink the cup that the Father has given me?" (John 18:11).

You may wonder why Judas' services were even necessary. After all, Jesus was likely the most recognizable Person in Jerusalem. The answer is that Jesus' cowardly foes were seeking a time to take Christ *in private*, lest they should instigate a riot (John 11:53–57). They wanted a secret arrest, followed by a secret trial, leading to a secret verdict. Hence, they avoided taking Him in the Temple where He taught, fittingly doing their dark work in the night (Matthew 26:55–56; Luke 22:6). Judas, whose treachery broke his own heart and damned his own soul, gave them just such an opportunity.

And yet, it was all unnecessary—the scheme, the soldiers, the swords. Jesus gave Himself over to them, willingly.

As the band of thugs arrested the unarmed and harmless Savior, He argued for His disciples' safety: "If you seek me, let these men go" (John 18:8). His selflessness knows no bounds.

We don't know how the soldiers responded, for Jesus' disciples ran off into the night, fleeing just as He had predicted (Matthew 26:31, 56). The Shepherd was smitten, and His tiny flock scattered (Zechariah 13:7b; John 16:32).

A. B. Bruce sees unbelief, not merely fear, in their flight:

> The sin lay not so much in the outward act, but in the inward state of mind of which it was the index. They fled in unbelief and despair, as men whose hope was blasted, from a man whose cause was lost, and whom God had abandoned to His enemies.[52]

They ran until the pain in their sides matched the pain in their consciences. Jesus' prophecy of their flight afflicted them. With the bread and wine of the New Covenant still on their breath, the disciples had abandoned the Savior.

> *Nothing I've done could merit God's grace;*
> *Nothing I'll do can take it away.*
> *I have one hope, in life and death:*
> *I have been clothed in Christ's righteousness.*
>
> *Nothing remains since Jesus has died;*
> *Justice was paid; the Judge satisfied.*
> *Great is my sin; greater His love;*
> *I have been cleansed with Calvary's blood!*
>
> *Christ is sufficient! His work is finished!*
> *He is my faith's Author and End;*
> *Christ is enough—my Savior and Friend!*[53]

---

52 Bruce, 467.

53 Chris Anderson and Greg Habegger, "Christ Is Sufficient" (Church Works Media, 2016).

DAY 14

JESUS BEFORE THE SANHEDRIN
Matthew 26:57–27:2

The first half of Jesus' final night before His crucifixion was spent with His friends. The latter half would be spent with His foes.

Two law-mocking trials consumed the hours between Gethsemane and Golgotha. As most in Jerusalem slept, Jesus endured a Jewish trial which included three hearings. And as most in Jerusalem greeted the morning, Jesus endured a Roman trial with yet three more hearings. In a real-life tragedy—complete with two acts of three scenes each—the Judge of sinners was presumptuously judged by sinners.

In the first religious trial, the Jews charged our Lord with blasphemy. It was a grueling, sleepless night for Jesus. He was seen first by Annas (the high priest Caiaphas' father-in-law; John 18:13, 19–24), apparently in an unofficial prehearing intended to satisfy the old man's vanity. Annas was the veritable "Godfather" of the high priesthood. He had held the position, then he passed it around to family members. The office was held "by not fewer than five of his sons, by his son-in-law Caiaphas, and by a grandson," historian Alfred Edersheim informs us.[54] Annas was a Sadducee, for whom religion was all power and no piety.

Next, Jesus was brought to the courtyard of Caiaphas' house (Matthew 26:57), where the true trial would commence. He would face the Sanhedrin itself in the second and most significant of the three hearings, the one on which Matthew focuses.

The Sanhedrin, comprised of religious leaders from various sects, was Israel's "Supreme Court." In this hastily assembled meeting,

---

54 Alfred Edersheim, *The Life and Times of Jesus the Messiah* (Peabody, MA: Hendrickson Publishers, 1993), 851.

they would serve as the prosecution, judge, and jury. The entire trial was a farce—an unlawful gathering, meeting at an unlawful hour, utilizing unlawful tactics. The initial questioning concerned Jesus' disciples and doctrine (John 18:19). As the proceedings stalled, the Sanhedrin bribed witnesses, but their testimonies were embarrassingly inconsistent (Matthew 26:59–61).

The accusers' desperate deception stands in stark contrast to Christ's silence. Though He had often spoken with such eloquent brilliance that His embarrassed questioners had skulked away (Matthew 22:15–46), now He made no answer (Matthew 26:62–63a). Just as He could have called for angelic deliverance in the garden, so He could have successfully defended Himself against the false charges. Instead, with only a few exceptions, He remained silent (Mark 14:61), submitting to unjust condemnation.

When He did speak, however, He seemed to intentionally implicate Himself, at least in the eyes of these wicked men. He was goaded by Caiaphas: "I adjure you by the living God, tell us if you are the Christ, the Son of God" (Matthew 27:63).

Jesus *was* the living God. He *was* the Christ. He *was* the Son of God. When He finally broke His silence, He did more than answer Caiaphas' presumptuous question. He affirmed His divine identity. But He also put the high priest and the high court on notice. With majestic poise He told His lying accusers that He would soon return to His Father's right hand. Furthermore, He would return to the Earth on the clouds of heaven—the King of kings and the Judge of all (Matthew 27:64; Mark 14:62). The tables, in time and eternity, would be turned.

With sickening theatrics, and in defiance of Leviticus 21:10, the high priest tore his garments. With unblushing gall, he charged Jehovah Himself with blasphemy (Matthew 27:65–66). By testifying of His own deity, Jesus had done for His accusers what they had been clumsily unable to do for themselves. They lacked evidence, credible witnesses, and even coherency. Yet, He bolstered their bogus charges, knowing full well that it would lead to His death.

DAY 14 — JESUS BEFORE THE SANHEDRIN

The seething pot of hatred and jealousy finally boiled over. Consumed with rage, the Sanhedrin behaved like brutes, beating the bound Messiah (Matthew 26:67–68; Luke 22:65). James Stalker marvels at the barbarity of Judaism's loftiest leaders: "One would wish to believe that it was only by the miserable underlings that such things were done; but the narrative makes it too clear that the masters led the way and the servants followed."[55]

They, the august and solemn Sanhedrin, spat on the One Whom they should have anointed. They mocked the One they should have adored. They viciously, hungrily beat the One before Whom they should have bowed—and before Whom they one day *will* bow. Yet, the Son of God absorbed their cruelty with stunning composure. The Almighty God allowed Himself to be beaten without retaliation.

Sweaty and flushed from their torture of Jesus, the Sanhedrin returned to order. They met for the third and final hearing at daybreak, a lame attempt to make their sham trial appear legal. Having found Jesus deserving of death, they sent Him to be judged by the civil magistrates, who alone had the power to execute a prisoner (Matthew 27:1). Many of these same men would ignore that technicality when Stephen was stoned some years later.

Jesus, condemned by the Jews, was led away to Pilate (Matthew 27:2), where more injustice awaited Him.

John MacArthur writes:

> [Jesus'] trial was unjust and illegal by virtually every principle of jurisprudence that was known at the time. Caiaphas and the Sanhedrin turned their own council into a kangaroo court with the predetermined purpose of killing Jesus. The trial they imposed on Him was one extended act of deliberate inhumanity, the greatest miscarriage of justice in the history of the world.[56]

---

55 James M. Stalker, *The Trial and Death of Jesus Christ: A Devotional History of Our Lord's Passion* (New York, NY: American Tract Society, 1894), 23.

56 MacArthur, *Murder*, 105.

Ah, but even here, Jesus was sovereign. God's eternal plan was being executed to perfection. The Sanhedrin—as guilty as they were—accomplished God's bidding. Acts 2:23 records the paradox: "This Jesus, delivered up according to the definite plan and foreknowledge of God, you crucified and killed by the hands of lawless men." Their plan to murder Jesus worked—as did God's plan to save sinners. Jesus' life wasn't taken from Him. It was given. *For us.*

> *Can it be? Who would believe?*
> *Our promised Prince lacked majesty:*
> *Stricken hard, grotesquely scarred—*
> *No face was e'er so cruelly marred.*
> *Ostracized, He was despised,*
> *As one from whom men hide their eyes.*
> *Beauty free—a brittle tree—*
> *Yet through Him God's strong arm we see!*
>
> *He was wounded, He was wounded!*
> *Praise our Servant Sacrifice!*
> *Hallelujah, Hallelujah!*
> *We are healed by Jesus' stripes!*[57]

~

---

57 Chris Anderson and Greg Habegger, "He Was Wounded (Isaiah 53)" (Church Works Media, 2010).

DAY

JESUS' MOCKERY AND BEATINGS
Matthew 26:67–68; 27:26; Luke 23:11–12

The cast of characters in the unfolding drama of Jesus' trials was as diverse as it was dastardly—villains even Dickens would be proud of. There were impious Jewish leaders, led by Annas and Caiaphas. There were pragmatic political leaders—Pilate and Herod—both as spineless as they were sinister. There were soldiers, brutes who delighted in pummeling a defenseless prisoner.

The entire series of events was undiluted evil, as Hugh Martin conveys: "The arrest was unprovoked: the accusation, false: the trial, a mockery: the evidence, perjury: the sentence, unrighteous and malicious: its execution, murder."[58]

J. C. Ryle presses into our minds the true humanity of the Lord Jesus, lest we minimize His sufferings:

> The catalogue of all the pains endured by our Lord's body, is indeed a fearful one.... The most savage tribes, in their refinement of cruelty, could hardly have heaped more agonizing tortures on an enemy than were heaped on the flesh and bones of our beloved Master. Never let it be forgotten that he had a real human body, a body exactly like our own, just as sensitive, just as vulnerable, just as capable of feeling intense pain.[59]

What moving words. When 1 Peter 3:18 says that "Christ ... suffered once for sins," the word *suffered* isn't merely a synonym for death. Christ *suffered*.

---

58 Hugh Martin, *The Shadow of Calvary* (Carlisle, PA: The Banner of Truth Trust, 2016), 22.

59 Ryle, *Expository Thoughts on Matthew*, 389.

Added to the physical brutality Jesus endured was the mental and emotional anguish inflicted by hours of monstrous mockery. We make a significant error if we take Jesus' quietness and refusal to revile His tormentors to mean that He didn't feel the sting of their barbs. Their verbal arrows hit their mark, and they hurt, as Psalm 69:20 foreshadowed: "Reproaches have broken my heart."

This barbaric torture of the Lord Jesus came in three waves. He was beaten by the Jews, beaten by the Romans, and finally crucified. Each phase was more painful and shameful than the last.

Jesus was mocked and beaten by the Jews.

We addressed Jesus' Jewish trials on Day 14. We noted that Jesus' claim to be the Son of God unleashed against Him a torrent of abuse. The Sanhedrin and their cronies rained down on Christ a storm of blows, marring His kind face (Matthew 26:67). They slapped Him and challenged Him to guess His afflicter. Most degrading of all, they spit in His face (Matthew 26:68), the universal sign of contempt. Spurgeon marvels at the undiluted evil of it all:

> If we want proof of the depravity of the heart of man, I will not point you to the stews of Sodom and Gomorrah, nor will I take you to the places where blood is shed in streams by wretches like to Herod and men of that sort. No, the clearest proof that man is utterly fallen, and that the natural heart is enmity against God, is seen in the fact that they did spit in Christ's face, did falsely accuse him, and condemn him, and lead him out as a malefactor, and hang him up as a felon that he might die upon a cross.[60]

We might justly adapt John 1:11 to read, "He came to His own, and His own spit in His face." But Jesus' abuse at the hands of the Jews was just the beginning.

---

60 Charles Spurgeon, "They Did Spit in His Face" in *Jesus, Keep Me Near the Cross: Experiencing the Passion and Power of Easter*, ed. Nancy Guthrie (Wheaton, IL: Crossway Books, 2009), 44–45.

DAY 15 — JESUS' MOCKERY AND BEATINGS

Jesus was mocked and beaten by the Romans.
The Jews marched Jesus to Pilate early in the morning. Pilate had political jurisdiction over southern Palestine. He would hear the initial charges, then send Jesus to Herod (who had authority in Galilee, in northern Palestine, see Day 18 in this devotional). Then it was back to Pilate for a third event, where Pilate would be forced by the Jews to render a judgment (see Day 19 in this devotional). Perhaps it's hard to follow the details of all Jesus' various trials. But the single thread that connected them? Violence.

First, Jesus was assailed by Herod's henchmen. Listen to Luke 23:11–12:

> And Herod with his soldiers treated him with contempt and mocked him. Then, arraying him in splendid clothing, he sent him back to Pilate. And Herod and Pilate became friends with each other that very day, for before this they had been at enmity with each other.

Jesus has been bringing evil men and women together for two millennia. They may hate each other, but they hate Jesus more. Herod and Pilate, generally rivals, united against Jesus—deriding Him, dressing Him like a king, and doing mock obeisance—a blasphemous motif that would only gain momentum in the hours to come.

Jesus' worst beatings came at the hands of Pilate, despite his vain attempts to wash them. Though Pilate knew Jesus was guiltless (Matthew 27:23), and though Pilate had been warned by his wife to "have nothing to do" with Jesus (Matthew 27:19), he was a servant to his career, to expediency, and thus to the Jewish mob. In a politically pragmatic gesture, Pilate twice offered to beat Jesus to placate the mob and save Jesus' life (Luke 23:15–16).

Ultimately, Pilate bowed to the brute force of the crowd's demands, scourging then crucifying the Lord Jesus (Mark 15:15).

This is the most stomach-churning portion of Jesus' sufferings. The Roman scourge is infamous, even now. The Lord Jesus' back and buttocks were laid bare. He was strapped to a waist-high post. And then he was whipped—*mutilated*—not with leather, but with a cat-o'-nine-tails, a whip weaponized with bits of bone, stone, and metal. His flesh was shredded. His bones were exposed. As Isaiah predicted some eight hundred years before it happened, "his appearance was so marred, beyond human semblance, and his form beyond that of the children of mankind" (Isaiah 52:14).

From the conclusion of the scourging, Jesus' appearance was more meat than man.

For their licentious levity, the soldiers again dressed Jesus in a scarlet robe. We get weak knees just imagining the agony of the fabric clinging to Jesus' lacerated back. The men one-upped Herod's gag, preparing a crown of thorns for Jesus' head and slamming it into His skull with a stick. Convulsing with laughter, they knelt before Him and hailed Him as the "King of the Jews"—a mockery both of Jesus and of His hated race (Matthew 27:27–31).

It is significant that thorns sprang up from the earth as a result of the Fall (Genesis 3:18). The very curse God pronounced against fallen humanity for the first sin, God Himself bore in these moments.

Jesus was mocked and crucified by sinners.

After the scourging, Jesus trudged to Calvary. Golgotha. The Skull.

By the time He was pinned to the cross, our Savior had already suffered an unimaginable sequence of agonies. The fact that He didn't incinerate His afflicters displays our Savior's unmatched meekness.

He was mocked. Pierced. Torn. Brutalized.

And He endured it in silence. The omnipotent God, embracing impotence, to save His fallen creation. What a marvel.

DAY 15 — JESUS' MOCKERY AND BEATINGS

Every knee shall bow to Thee,
Precious Lamb Who bowed for me.
No more shall they kneel in scorn;
No more shall Thy crown be thorns. [61]

∽

My Jesus, fair, was pierced by thorns,
By thorns grown from the fall.
Thus He who gave the curse was torn
To end that curse for all. [62]

∽

---

61 Chris Anderson and Molly Ijames, "Every Knee Shall Bow" (Church Works Media, 2012).

62 Chris Anderson and Greg Habegger, "My Jesus, Fair" (Church Works Media, 2008).

DAY 16

JESUS' POWER AND PETER'S WEAKNESS
Matthew 26:57–75

The records of Jesus' trials and Peter's denials are intertwined in the four Gospels. Matthew seems to intentionally contrast them, moving from Christ (26:57), to Peter (26:58), back to Christ (26:59–68), then back again to Peter (26:69–75), before finally settling our attention on Jesus (chapter 27). The comparison isn't flattering for the audacious disciple.

Peter's failure was spectacular. To appreciate the depth of his fall, we must remember what had transpired in the hours preceding it. He had argued with Jesus, insisting that he would remain with Him unto death, even if all others denied Him (Matthew 26:31–35). The ease with which he elevated himself above his companions is troubling: *"You and I both know, Lord, that these other guys are sketchy. But not me. I'll die before denying You."*

Immediately after his empty boasts, he had slept when he should have prayed, ignoring both Christ's need and Christ's warnings (Matthew 26:40–41). He had displayed misguided zeal by severing Malchus' ear (Matthew 26:51). He had then forsaken Jesus and run for his life, fulfilling our Lord's sad prophecy (Matthew 26:56).

Now, Peter does deserve some credit. Unlike the other disciples, he and John collected their courage and followed Jesus to Caiaphas' home, albeit at a distance (Mark 14:54). No doubt Peter had convinced himself that he would do better if another opportunity arose.

Not so. Whereas he promised Christ that he would stand out from the other disciples for uncommon valor, he instead distinguished himself by uncommon shame. He denied Christ before the servant girl who gave him entrance to Caiaphas' grounds (Matthew 26:69–70). Mark 14:68 indicates that the rooster crowed after this first denial—a warning shot, if you will. Peter moved into the courtyard, away from the light of the fire by which he had warmed himself. Still, he was recognized in the shadows, this time by several others who were sacrificing their sleep to leer as Jesus' scandal unfolded. Again Peter denied knowing Jesus, this time reinforcing his words with a vow (Matthew 26:71–72).

And during all this, Christ's mockery and beatings had commenced (Mark 14:64–66). Charles Swindoll reminds us of the juxtaposition of Jesus' suffering and Peter's shame:

> Jesus was tormented, humiliated, spit upon, cursed, and falsely accused. He stood there silent and bleeding. Then they began to mock Him. They blindfolded Him and slapped His face, challenging Him to "Prophesy! Tell us who hit you!" And off in the shadows, taking it all in, stood frightened Peter, haunted by the memory of his own words.[63]

Peter was identified a third time, now with the evidence of his Galilean speech and the testimony of a relative of Malchus brought against him (John 18:26). Desperate with fear, Peter renounced his Lord even more vehemently, accentuating his denials with a series of curses (Matthew 26:74).

This third denial coincided with the shrill crowing of the rooster. Peter looked across the courtyard and locked eyes with Jesus (Matthew 26:75; Luke 22:61). How devastating the gaze of the bloodied Savior must have been! Surely, His bruised and swollen eyes communicated grief and pity, not disgust. But such love can be harder to bear than anger. Broken, Peter fled again, this time seeking to escape his own thoughts, not a garden arrest (Matthew 26:75).

Though we are prone to condemn Peter, honesty forces us to see our own failures in his. Despite our confidence—and even our genuine

---

63 Charles Swindoll, *The Darkness and the Dawn: Empowered by the Tragedy and Triumph of the Cross* (Nashville, TN: Word Publishing, 2001), 48.

love for Christ—our flesh is heartbreakingly weak. We too have known the frustration of sinning, then determining again and again to try harder and do better, only to fail again, more despicably than ever. We know how such failure can breed despair. We know shame.

But we also learn from our brother Peter that failure need not be final. In fact, Scripture dares us to hope for Peter in the last phrase of Matthew 26: "He went out and wept bitterly." Bravado dissolved to sorrow. And there's *hope* in sorrow. "A broken and contrite heart, O God, you will not despise" (Psalm 51:17). We've been there.

Peter, though shamed and humbled, would not be utterly lost—not like Judas. Why? Because Jesus had prayed for him (Luke 22:31–32).

The Lord Jesus had predicted that Peter would falter. But He had also predicted that Peter would rise again and be used to rally the other disciples who shared his frailty and needed his help (Luke 22:31–32). The righteous man, we read in Proverbs 24:16, is not one who never stumbles; he is one who doesn't stay down when he stumbles, even if he falls seven times.

After Jesus' resurrection, Peter was recommissioned to ministry by our Lord's very pointed, very gracious words (John 21:15–17). Though Peter had considered forsaking the ministry and returning to his fishing career, Jesus wasn't finished with him. He allowed Peter to replace his three denials with three affirmations of love. And He gave Peter work to do. Just as He had commanded Peter to fish for men three years earlier, He now commanded him, three times, "Feed my sheep." And Peter did.

After Jesus' resurrection and the outpouring of the Holy Spirit, Peter's pride gave way to humility (1 Peter 5:1–5). The author of 1 Peter bears no resemblance to the brash man we see in the four Gospels. Further, Peter's cowardice gave way to seemingly boundless courage. He stared down the very Sanhedrin that murdered Jesus, denounced their crimes, and preached Christ with unflinching boldness (Acts 4:8–13, 19–20; 5:29–32).

Jesus did that. Through a convicting look, through a triumphant resurrection, through a compassionate restoration, and through the sending of the Spirit—*Jesus* did that work in Peter. He delights to forgive and change frail Christians.

We too, once emptied of our wicked self-reliance, can know the forgiving and enabling grace of the Savior, the same grace that restored the fallen disciple and transformed his stubborn character. We too can learn from our frailty to abandon every hope except the transforming gospel of Jesus Christ.

Martin Luther—a kindred spirit to Peter if ever there was one—found great gospel hope in Jesus' reclamation of the impetuous disciple. He writes,

> No article of the Creed is so hard to believe as this: I believe in the forgiveness of sins. But look at Peter. If I could paint a portrait of Peter, I would write on every hair of his head forgiveness of sins.[64]

> *I run to Christ when stalked by sin*
> *And find a sure escape.*
> *"Deliver me," I cry to Him;*
> *Temptation yields to grace.*

> *I run to Christ when plagued by shame*
> *And find my one defense.*
> *"I bore God's wrath," He pleads my case—*
> *My Advocate and Friend.*[65]

---

64 Quoted in John A. Broadus, *Commentary on Matthew* (Grand Rapids, MI: Kregel Publications, 1990), 554.

65 Chris Anderson and Greg Habegger, "I Run to Christ" (Church Works Media, 2010).

DAY

JESUS' BETRAYER

Matthew 27:1–10; John 13:18–19, 21–30; Acts 1:15–25

The biblical record of the hours leading up to Christ's sacrifice is precious, if somewhat hard to read. One could wonder, then, why Scripture even momentarily takes our attention away from Jesus to tell of His betrayer. Yet, this is precisely what it does, recording for us the culmination of Judas' tragic life. As Christ's death provides the sinner with hope, Judas' death provides the sinner with an unforgettable warning.

While Judas' deed was a shock to his fellow disciples, it was no sudden decision. The apostle John—shortly after telling us of the Jewish leaders' desire to arrest Jesus in a place of privacy (John 11:53, 57)—informs us that Judas was the disciples' treasurer, and a dishonest one at that (John 12:6). He was indignant at the "waste" of Mary's lavish gift to the Lord Jesus (John 12:5)—a heartbreaking insult to Christ and a loathsome look into Judas' own heart. Judas slouched into his devilry over time. Those who hear the truth are never unchanged by it. The same sun which thaws snow, hardens clay. Judas had three years of listening to Jesus—and the frightening effect was a hardened heart and deadened conscience.

His thievery was audacious. His betrayal was revolting. His desecration of Jesus' sanctuary of prayer in the garden was grossly irreverent. The fact that he stabbed Jesus in the back even as he kissed His face was maddening. Indeed, "the kisses of an enemy are deceitful" (Proverbs 27:6 KJV).

James M. Stalker comments ably on the duplicity embodied in Judas' kiss and of its effect on the Savior:

> It was a sin against the human heart and all its charities. But none can feel its horror as it must have been felt by Jesus. That

night and the next day His face was marred in many ways: it was furrowed by the bloody sweat; it was bruised with blows; they spat upon it; it was rent with thorns: but nothing went so close to His heart as the profanation of this kiss.[66]

Jesus was unsurprised by Judas' treachery. He predicted it in the upper room, probably to protect the disciples from despair once it happened (John 13:18–19, 21–30). Indeed, the Scriptures predicted Judas' betrayal one thousand years before the cursed kiss (Psalm 41:9).

Nevertheless, the record of Judas' final fall is chilling. John 13:27 tells us, with utter candor, that "Satan entered into him." Such a mission was too vital to entrust to the devil's minions, so he took on the work himself—and relished it. There is an apparent double meaning in John's record of Judas' departure from the upper room and descent into physical and spiritual darkness: "And it was night" (John 13:30).

Judas' wicked deed was immediately followed by regret. When the sale of Jesus was complete, his conscience was pricked—perhaps by Christ's calm response to His betrayal, His healing of Malchus, or His silent endurance of the violent persecution. Some have suggested that Judas was attempting to force Jesus to defend Himself and forsake His apparent passivity. Whatever his motivation had been, in the wake of the betrayal, Judas was shocked by his own wretchedness.

Jesus had once asked, "What shall a man give in return for his soul?" (Matthew 16:26). For Judas, the answer had been thirty pieces of silver—a miserable bargain.

Judas suffocated beneath his guilt. He grieved, but grief alone wouldn't atone for his sin (2 Corinthians 7:10). He bore witness to his co-conspirators of Jesus' innocence (Matthew 27:4), confessing his sin, but not to God. He even returned the dreaded silver, as though doing so could salve his conscience or undo his crime

---

66 Stalker, 4.

(Matthew 27:5a). What a sobering example of the human experience: the forbidden object which we determine to acquire at any cost not only leaves us dissatisfied, but soon becomes loathsome to us. Though sorrowful, Judas found no redemption, for there is no salvation outside of the Christ he had betrayed (Acts 4:12).

Judas had his moment. For a brief time, he had led a "great crowd." For a few fleeting minutes, he had been admired. Yet, he spent his final moments on Earth utterly alone. Though provoked to sin by a host of tempters, and though indwelt by Satan himself, once the deed was done, Judas was discarded. He regretted his betrayal—*alone*. He died a gruesome death—*alone* (Matthew 27:5; Acts 1:18). And now he suffers in hell—*alone*. Scripture tells us that Judas went "to his own place" (Acts 1:26)—a place of eternal damnation. Truly, as Jesus remarked, "It would have been better for that man if he had not been born" (Matthew 26:24).

The priests' neglect of Judas' soul was outdistanced only by their hypocrisy with his silver (Matthew 27:3–4). Though they were glad to pay a bribe and condemn the Son of God, they piously refused to take back the blood money with which they had purchased their prize (Matthew 27:6). They tacitly admitted their own guilt, and their sudden scrupulousness is obnoxious.

Having schemed the murder of the Messiah, they sanctimoniously used the silver to buy a field to bury indigents (Matthew 27:5–8)— "straining out a gnat and swallowing a camel" (Matthew 23:24). Yet, even in this, they unwittingly fulfilled biblical prophecy (Zechariah 11:13; Matthew 27:9–10). Even their treachery was part of God's plan of redemption. As John MacArthur writes, "God remains absolutely sovereign over all, even when it seems the most evil schemes of sinful men are about to achieve a sinister success."[67]

Moralists would do well to learn from wicked Judas. We can no more atone for our own sins than he did. Could regret, or confession to priests, or almsgiving purchase heaven, Judas would be there now.

---

67   MacArthur, *Murder*, 21.

But he is not. He stands as a sobering testimony of unrepentant sin and its horrible end. In the words of J. C. Ryle, "Let us remember Judas, and beware. He is set up before us as a beacon. Let us look well at him, and not make shipwreck."[68]

So weary of our trait'rous flesh—
Of sin we hate, yet crave—
We yearn to see temptation's death,
Indwelling sin's dark grave.

Come quickly, Lord! Make all things new!
Redeem the church, Your bride.
With longing eyes we look for You,
For home is at Your side![69]

---

68 Ryle, *Expository Thoughts on Matthew*, 384.
69 Chris Anderson and Greg Habegger, "Come Quickly, Lord" (Church Works Media, 2008).

DAY 18

JESUS BEFORE HEROD
Luke 23:1–12; John 18:29–38

As the sun He created rose over Jerusalem, our weary Lord was led by the religious thugs to Pontius Pilate. So began the civil trial in which the accusation was changed from blasphemy (which mattered little to Rome) to insurrection. It was a shrewd move. The Jews knew that Pilate, the harsh and calculating governor of Judea under Tiberius Caesar, feared revolution. Ever fastidious about making themselves unclean, especially during the Passover, the Jews refused to enter Pilate's palace, the Praetorium, requiring him to speak to them from a balcony (John 18:28).

Like the Jewish trial, the civil trial proceeded in three phases.

Pilate's first view of Christ must have been striking. The Jews, who so often complained of Roman abuses, delivered to Pilate a man whose face was swollen, bruised, and bloody. Though Matthew's account deals with the initial hearing only briefly (27:11), John's unpacks it more specifically (18:29–38). Pilate first asked the nature of the charge, and the Jews were deliberately evasive. Pilate then pursued the matter himself through a personal interview with Christ. He was unimpressed by the religious controversy and said as much to both Jesus and the Jews.

Still, the Jews persisted, desiring the death sentence which they themselves could not deliver. They added the false charge that Christ forbade the paying of taxes (Luke 23:2). Now *that* was blasphemous to Rome! Still, Pilate essentially acquitted the accused: "I find no guilt in him" (John 18:38; Luke 23:4). The sentence thus delivered, Christ should have been released. However, hoping to avoid the Jews' displeasure, and having learned that Jesus was from Galilee,

Pilate sent Him to be tried by Herod—Pilate's first attempt to shirk his duty, but certainly not his last (Luke 23:5–7).

Herod Antipas, like his murderous father Herod the Great, was a wretch. He was notoriously immoral, and when John the Baptist called him out on his immorality, he took John's head (Luke 23:8–9). Jesus had called John the Baptist the best of men (Matthew 11:11). And John was killed by the worst of men.

Herod was pleased by the opportunity to meet Jesus, for he had longed to see the Miracle-Worker for some time (Luke 9:9; 23:8). Frankly, he hoped to see a magic trick, but he would be disappointed. Jesus had no miracles to perform for the fop. Nor were Herod's questions any more successful in getting Jesus to engage. Whereas Jesus gave at least brief answers to the Sanhedrin and to Pilate, He stonewalled Herod (Luke 23:9). But the Jewish leaders had made the trip, and with Herod looking on, they continued to accuse Jesus (Luke 23:10).

Herod found the entire affair to be a great bore. Disinterested in the accusations from the Jews and unable to provoke a response from the Savior, Herod and his men determined to amuse themselves. They battered and bullied Jesus. Finally, Herod came up with what he considered to be a deliciously funny idea. He wrapped his rival "King of the Jews" in royal garments—making Jesus a veritable clown—and sent Him back to Pilate (Luke 23:10–12). In reality, Herod himself was the clown; Geldenhuys notes, "And thus Herod sends Him back to Pilate without making the slightest attempt to investigate His case judicially."[70]

Pilate was likely disappointed to see the buck passed back to him. But he couldn't resist a chuckle at Herod's prank. United in their tomfoolery during history's most tragic event, the former rivals became fast friends. Nevertheless, the second hearing ended like the first: Pilate and Herod affirmed Christ's innocence (Luke 23:13–16).

---

70 Norval Geldenhuys, *Commentary on the Gospel of Luke: The English Text with Introduction, Exposition, and Notes* (Grand Rapids, MI: William B. Eerdmans Publishing Company, 1993), 594.

DAY 18 — JESUS BEFORE HEROD

Political rulers have rarely been friends to Christ or Christians. And yet, they are powerless to oppose God's plan. Indeed, they are pawns in it. And so, several months after Jesus' ascension, in response to ongoing persecution, the infant church offered a prayer that referenced Herod and Pilate as notorious villains and framed their sinful rebellion as a fulfillment of Psalm 2:

> Sovereign Lord, who made the heaven and the earth and the sea and everything in them, who through the mouth of our father David, your servant, said by the Holy Spirit,
>
>> "Why did the Gentiles rage,
>> and the peoples plot in vain?
>> The kings of the earth set themselves,
>> and the rulers were gathered together,
>> against the Lord and against his Anointed" [Psalm 2:1–2]—
>
> For truly in this city there were gathered together against your holy servant Jesus, whom you anointed, both Herod and Pontius Pilate, along with the Gentiles and the peoples of Israel, to do whatever your hand and your plan had predestined to take place. (ACTS 4:24–28)

All of those involved in the trials and subsequent crucifixion— Herod, Pilate, Jews, and Gentiles alike—had formed an unholy alliance against the Messiah. And it has always been so: former rivals unite in their shared hatred of Jesus. But while these villains fulfilled a plan they had devised *for years*, they accomplished a plan which God had devised *from eternity*.

Herod and Pilate snickered for a moment. But their mirth was short-lived. As J. Dwight Pentecost relates, both men "were to be stripped of their power and to die in shameful exile."[71]

The Almighty has reserved the last laugh for Himself (Psalm 2:4).

---

[71] J. Dwight Pentecost, *The Words and Works of Jesus Christ: A Study of the Life of Christ* (Grand Rapids, MI: Zondervan Publishing House, 1981), 535. Ironically, it was the unbridled ambition of his unlawful wife, Herodias—who required John the Baptist's head—that eventually led to Herod's ruin. See Geldenhuys, 600–01.

Almighty laughs as nations rage!
Our self-proclaimed "enlightened" age
May scorn and cast off sacred rules,
But God derides delusive fools.
His reign depends not on our whim;
We neither aid nor threaten Him.
Almighty bids us, "Kiss the Son,
Or by His anger be undone."

Almighty lives and cannot change;
Men rise and fall like crashing waves.
Their boasting is but vanity;
Man is no match for Deity.
The righteous live in endless day,
But fools, like chaff, blow soon away.
Almighty rules unruly men,
Who, though they scoff, will answer Him. [72]

---

[72] Chris Anderson and Paul Keew, "God Supreme" (Church Works Media, 2015).

DAY

19

JESUS BEFORE PILATE

Matthew 27:11–26; Luke 23:1–5; John 18:28–19:16

We have followed the Lord Jesus from Pilate's Praetorium, to Herod, and now back to Pilate. The final appearance before Pilate—the third of the Roman trials—receives the most attention in Scripture (Matthew 27:12–26; John 19:1–16).

I described Pilate as a Dickens-type villain. Listen to Giuseppe Ricciotti's description:

> The historians Philo and Flavius Josephus, and the Gospels all mention Pilate, and the very least all three sources tell us is that he was a cantankerous and stubborn man, violent, extortionate, and tyrannical in government.... It is certain that Pilate was not a successful procurator. He not only hated the Jewish people but he felt a compelling need to show them his hatred.[73]

Whatever Pilate's other vices, on this particular day his most striking character quality was utter cowardice. And while he certainly hated the Jews, on this day they bested him.

Despite finding Jesus innocent of any capital crime—twice (Luke 23:4, 14–15; John 18:38)—Pilate continued to hold Jesus under arrest. In the immediate aftermath of declaring Jesus guiltless, he bargained with the Jews, offering to pacify them by having Jesus beaten (Luke 23:16).

The Jews were in no mood for a beating—they wanted blood. They pressed Pilate further, demanding crucifixion, and for a third time, Pilate protested Jesus' innocence: "Why? What evil has He done? I have found in him no guilt deserving death" (Luke 23:22a).

---

73 Giuseppe Ricciotti, *Life of Christ*, trans. Alba I. Zizzamia, ed. Aloysius Croft (Milwaukee, WI: The Bruce Publishing Company, 1952), 22.

The declaration of Jesus' innocence was immediately followed by another offer to beat Him (Luke 23:22b). His willingness to beat an innocent man to pacify a mob tells you everything you need to know about Pontius Pilate.

At this point in the narrative, we are introduced to two interesting facts. First, we are told that Pilate recognized that the Jews were motivated purely by envy (Matthew 27:18). Second, we are told that Pilate's somewhat superstitious wife had had a dream about Jesus which was making her anxious that very day. She urged her husband, "Have nothing to do with that righteous man" (Matthew 27:19). Pilate should have listened.

Instead, recognizing that the mob's bloodlust was unabated, he sought another loophole: He offered to release to the people a prisoner as a show of goodwill, per a Passover custom. Again, his maneuvering was frustrated, for the mob chose the murderer Barabbas over the sinless Savior (Matthew 27:15–21). Step by pragmatic step, Pilate had succeeded only in making the hated Jews his "rulers."

As the crowd cried out for Jesus to be crucified, Pilate appealed to them—yet again!—that Jesus was innocent (John 19:4, 6). Reading his verdicts in succession is startling:

> I find no guilt in him. (John 18:38)
>
> I did not find this man guilty of any of your charges against him. Neither did Herod, for he sent him back to us. Look, nothing deserving death has been done by him. (Luke 23:14–15)
>
> Why [crucify him]? What evil has he done? (Matthew 27:23)
>
> I have found in him no guilt deserving death. (Luke 23:22)
>
> I find no guilt in him.... I find no guilt in him. (John 19:4, 6)

Pilate wanted to let Jesus go. It almost seems that he wanted to *believe*. But not enough. His intrigue never turned to repentance.

DAY 19 — JESUS BEFORE PILATE

A. T. Robertson dismisses Pilate's questions as "a feeble protest by a flickering conscience."[74]

You almost pity Pilate, though you know he was a scoundrel. He really did want to do the right thing—as long as it wouldn't cost him anything. He appealed to the Jews. And on several occasions, he appealed to Jesus. Their brief interactions are fascinating.

In John 18:33–38, on their first meeting, Pilate heard Jesus say that He is a King, but that His Kingdom is "not of this world." Jesus emphasized that He had come into the world to bear witness to the truth, to which Pilate famously (and rather dismissively) replied, "What is truth?"

Then in Matthew 27:12–14, Pilate asked Jesus if He had heard all the slanderous accusations made against Him. Jesus made no reply.

John 19:9–11 records their final, riveting conversation:

> [Pilate] entered his headquarters again and said to Jesus, "Where are you from?" But Jesus gave him no answer. So Pilate said to him, "You will not speak to me? Do you not know that I have authority to release you and authority to crucify you?" Jesus answered him, "You would have no authority over me at all unless it had been given you from above."

God had granted authority to Pilate over Jesus in this single instance. And Pilate had essentially given that authority to the Jews. Paralyzed by his own fear and selfishness, the governor was governed—by a mob.

Ironically, the Jews who had accused the peaceful Savior of insurrection were themselves on the verge of rioting, and Pilate knew it. Despite declaring Jesus to be innocent *five separate times*, Pilate ultimately caved. He delivered Jesus to be crucified (Matthew 27:23–26).

---

74 A. T. Robertson, *Word Pictures in the New Testament* (Nashville, TN: Broadman Press, 1930), 1:227.

In the end, Pilate washed his hands of the matter—literally. He yielded to the Jews' desire for Jesus' crucifixion, but only after symbolically excusing himself by theatrically washing his hands and pronouncing, "I am innocent of this man's blood; see to it yourselves" (Matthew 27:24).

No, Pilate. You're not innocent. Not then and not now.

In fact, there are two mortals mentioned in the regal *Apostle's Creed.* One is Mary, the mother of Jesus. The other is Pontius Pilate, the spineless villain. His washed hands, like Lady Macbeth's, are bloody still.

> *I waged a war against the Lord,*
> *A war I could not win—*
> *I sought to spurn His ev'ry word,*
> *And smote Him with my sin.*
> *I hurled defiance like a spear,*
> *Rebellion like a stone;*
> *I fought the One I should have feared,*
> *And raged at Heaven's throne.*
>
> *But O, how great the Savior's grace*
> *To pity one who had spit in His face!*
> *And O, what love I owe this God*
> *Who bought my peace with His own precious blood!*
>
> *God waged a war against my soul,*
> *A war that I had earned—*
> *Perdition was rebellion's toll;*
> *His wrath against me burned;*
> *And yet His mercy would not cease*
> *Despite the scorn I'd shown;*
> *He willed to win a costly peace*
> *And claim me as His own.*

DAY 19 — JESUS BEFORE PILATE

God waged a war against Himself,
A war He fought and won—
The wrath which hovered o'er my head
He spent upon His Son.
My Foe was shrouded in my sin
Then tortured and reviled;
My Lord was torn by God and men,
And I am reconciled![75]

∼

---

75 Chris Anderson and Greg Habegger, "I Waged a War" (Church Works Media, 2025).

DAY 20

JESUS AND THE FRENZIED MOB
Matthew 27:15–26; John 19:12–16

Proverbs 12:18 teaches us that "rash words are like sword thrusts."

The Jewish mob's intense hatred of Jesus, egged on by their wicked spiritual leaders, led them to a series of rash statements. They hated Pilate. They hated Caesar. They hated Rome. But their obsessive hatred of Jesus drove them to a series of blasphemies. We will consider three.

They preferred a murderer to the Messiah.

Pilate's interaction with the Jews reads like a chess match. Pilate and the Jewish leaders made moves and counter moves, trying to force their opponents into an error. Ironically, it was Pilate who wanted to protect Jesus, whereas Jesus' own people were delirious in their desire for His death. "He came to his own, and his own people did not receive him" (John 1:11).

Pilate tried to avoid a direct confrontation with the Jews. He continually looked for an easy out—from sending Jesus to Herod to beating an innocent man to offering to release a prisoner. Each time, Pilate greatly underestimated his opponents. It's the last of Pilate's failed maneuvers we'll consider here.

There was a tradition in Judea associated with the Passover feast. As a sign of goodwill, the governor would release a criminal. Desperate to free Jesus without enraging the Jews, Pilate offered to release Him in fulfillment of this custom. It was a lame attempt. Pilate was playing checkers, not chess (Matthew 27:15–23).

Pilate gave the Jews two options. He offered to release a notorious criminal named Barabbas—a man so violently dangerous that Pilate was certain they would decline him. As the other option, he offered

Jesus, the meek and lowly Healer and Teacher. *"Surely this reasonable crowd will see the danger of releasing a madman like Barabbas,"* he reasoned. And he was wrong.

The Jewish leaders instructed the people to choose the wicked man over the righteous. Without hesitation, the crowd called for Barabbas. They preferred a murderer to their Messiah. They embodied Proverbs 17:15: "He who justifies the wicked and he who condemns the righteous are both alike an abomination to the Lord."

But here's the thing. Hidden in this Passion narrative is a gospel gem—an analogy of salvation. Barabbas was wicked. He should have been crucified on the center cross. But he was released, and the guiltless Son of God died instead—on the cross that should have belonged to Barabbas.

Do you see it? You're Barabbas. We're all Barabbas. We all deserve condemnation. And by the grace of God, by the blood of Jesus, we are set free.

The Jews are guilty of making a wicked choice. But Barabbas' being set free while Jesus was condemned is instructive. It reminds us of the very grace that saves us.

They bowed the knee to Caesar rather than to Christ.

The Jews' second blasphemy again comes in response to Pilate. The early morning had fled, and the sun began to burn down on the scene. Pilate, still determined to release Jesus, was overwhelmed by the Jewish mob's railings about Jesus. With one voice they shouted, again and again, "Crucify him! Crucify him!" (John 19:15a). Exasperated, and foolish, Pilate inquired, "Shall I crucify your King?" They responded—astoundingly—"We have no king but Caesar!" (John 19:15b). It was an echo of an earlier argument: "If you release this man, you are not Caesar's friend. Everyone who makes himself a king opposes Caesar" (John 19:12).

They knew what buttons to push. Checkmate. Pilate was beaten. "So he delivered him over to them to be crucified" (John 19:16).

DAY 20 — JESUS AND THE FRENZIED MOB

The Jews won. But they had sold their souls. Edersheim writes, "With this cry Judaism was, in the person of its representatives, guilty of denial of God, of blasphemy, of apostasy."[76]

And it would get worse.

They called for Jesus' blood to be held against them and their children.

As if the Jews had not already implicated themselves enough, they basically dared God to bring down swift judgment on their heads. When Pilate—spinelessly, vainly—washed his hands to cleanse himself of Jesus' blood, the Jews made a brash and fatal vow: "And all the people answered, 'His blood be on us and on our children!'" (Matthew 27:25).

Remember the proverb with which we began this section: "Rash words are like sword thrusts" (Proverbs 12:18). I'm not certain that rasher words were ever spoken. The Jews called down God's judgment for Jesus' death on themselves. Worse, they called down God's judgment on their own children. What a foolish, wicked, reckless thing to say.

Jesus was delivered to be crucified. The Jews got their wish. But His death was all part of God's eternal plan. And He would live again.

Jerusalem, however, was finished. A generation later, in A.D. 70, the Romans laid waste to it, as Jesus had predicted (Matthew 23:27–24:2). The Jews' rebellion finally pushed them over the edge. The Holy City was razed. And the Jews' rash vow was fulfilled, *on their children*.

Acts 5:28 provides a bit of irony in this tragic story. After Jesus' resurrection and ascension, as the Jerusalem church was thriving, the same Sanhedrin that had enraged the mob and ultimately crucified Christ complained to Peter and John: "You intend to bring this man's blood upon us." *Do you think?!* What short memories they had. Or rather, how capricious they were. But it was too late. They had brought Jesus' blood on themselves.

---

76 Edersheim, *Times*, 851.

Studying Jesus' suffering is sobering. But observing the step-by-step destruction of the Jews is sobering as well. The Lord Jesus came to save them, not condemn them (John 3:17). He was the Messiah promised throughout the entire Old Testament, as far back as Eden (Genesis 3:15). He came to save *them*.

But sin makes people stupid. Reckless. Hellbent.

And the frenzied mob blasphemed themselves into utter damnation. Checkmate.

> *Why should heathen mock the Lord?*
> *"Where is He?" their scoffing word.*
> *In the heav'ns He reigns alone,*
> *Ruling from His lofty throne.*
> *What He pleases, He performs;*
> *All to His design conforms.*
> *Not to us, but to our King,*
> *Honor, praise, and glory bring!*[77]

~

---

77 Chris Anderson and George Elvey, "Not to Us (Psalm 115)" (Church Works Media, 2010).

DAY 21

JESUS' JOURNEY TO GOLGOTHA
Luke 23:26–31

It was around nine o'clock in the morning when the trial concluded and the execution commenced (Mark 15:25). Already marred beyond recognition, the Savior lumbered toward Calvary, where the beating and blasphemy which He had borne through the night would climax in His crucifixion.

Jesus' Death March

It was customary for the condemned to carry their own crosses. Jesus began to do so, staggering down Jerusalem's narrow streets. The brutality of the last several hours took its toll, and Jesus succumbed to the weight of the cross, unable to continue. A man named Simon of Cyrene was plucked from the crowd and forced to help Jesus carry His cross. This little assistance only facilitated Jesus' suffering; each bloody step took Him nearer to Golgotha.

Simon of Cyrene has been the subject of much speculation. He was likely an immigrant to Palestine from Cyrene, modern-day Libya. It is also likely—or at least *hoped*—that his exposure to Christ on this dreadful day brought him to salvation. Why would John Mark describe Simon as "the father of Alexander and Rufus" unless those men were known to the Christian community (Mark 15:21)? Paul's greeting sent to a Rufus who lived in Rome, along with his godly mother, adds to the likelihood of this story, though we can't be certain (Romans 16:13).

Jesus' death march wasn't long. The winding Via Dolorosa (or *Sorrowful Way*) in Jerusalem is a short street—only six hundred feet long, approximately two blocks in some of our cities. Its supposed "stations of the cross" are apocryphal. Still, walking that route, even today, is sobering. It is certain that Jesus was forced to stumble from the Praetorium to Calvary, though the precise path cannot be known. But I've walked those streets, and it's not hard to imagine the crowds, the trail of blood, and our exhausted and expiring Savior.

The triumphal entry, less than a week earlier, was a distant memory. The city which had welcomed Jesus with shouts and songs and palm branches now expelled Him. He would die outside of Jerusalem proper, as Jewish laws required (Leviticus 24:14). Hebrews makes much of this fact, that Jesus suffered "outside the camp" (Hebrews 13:11–13), using the phrase as a call for Christians to be willing to be rejected by the culture as they identify with Christ.

Jesus' Mourners

The four Gospels could give the impression that the entire Jewish population was united in its hatred for the Lord Jesus. But Luke alone describes "a great multitude of the people and of women who were mourning and lamenting for him" (Luke 23:27). Most of these people—some believers, some not—probably awakened to the news that Jesus had been tried and convicted while they slept. We can imagine them praying that the news was false, rushing into the Jerusalem streets, and witnessing a scene that must have seemed incomprehensible. The kind, compassionate Healer and Teacher—the very One many believed to be their Messiah—was staggering out of the city. Had the mob not been shouting His name, these mourners would not have recognized Him. He was headed for Calvary, and His death was already certain.

Jesus' Warning

A group of women—not Jesus' mother or close companions, but perhaps professional mourners[78]—wept for Him. In incomparable selflessness, Jesus summoned the energy to mourn for *them* in return. And He urged them to consider their own spiritual peril. His lament is selfless and chilling:

---

78 So says John MacArthur, *The MacArthur New Testament Commentary: Luke 18–24* (Chicago, IL: Moody Publishers, 2014), 370.

Daughters of Jerusalem, do not weep for me, but weep for yourselves and for your children. For behold, the days are coming when they will say, "Blessed are the barren and the wombs that never bore and the breasts that never nursed!" Then they will begin to say to the mountains, "Fall on us," and to the hills, "Cover us." For if they do these things when the wood is green, what will happen when it is dry? (Luke 23:28–31)

That's a lot, especially considering that Jesus was in the process of dying when He said it—too weary to carry His own cross and likely in shock from the brutalities He had already suffered. The fact that He was so coherent and so compassionate defies understanding.

Jesus was once again reciting Scripture, this time quoting a prophecy of judgment from Zechariah 12:10–14, where the Jews realize they have murdered their own Messiah. Jesus anticipated a time when sinners would be *judged* rather than rendering perverse judgments. Remarkably, He described the coming condemnation of the Jews not with relish or a desire for revenge, but with profound sorrow. His words on the Via Dolorosa were the last of several lamentations over Jerusalem (Luke 19:41–44; Matthew 23:37–39), warning these women of the judgment coming to their people. Once again, we are confronted with Jesus' love for those who abused Him.

But we are also struck with the horrific scenes He predicted. He spoke of a time when women *without* children will be grateful—an absolute turnabout from what is expected, and thus a description of catastrophic troubles. He spoke of a time when people will be praying for the mountains to mercifully put them out of their misery.

He likely was describing the fall of Jerusalem in A.D. 70, an event Josephus depicts in horrific detail (cf. Luke 21:20–24). But Jesus was probably also looking beyond that point—prophesying the final judgment of the wicked. The fact that Revelation 6:16 uses the same imagery of people crying out to the mountains to hide them from the wrath of Christ bolsters this likelihood.

Jesus' final lines to these ladies are tragic, and a bit difficult to interpret. The likely meaning, I believe, is this: "If they do these things when the wood is green"—*if God has allowed such severe judgment to fall on Me, the Innocent*—"what will happen when it is dry"—*it is certain that God will not spare the wicked who have carried out this evil.* Jesus was urging the sorrowful women to consider their own souls—to believe in Him as Savior, not just to pity Him for His sufferings. To bring back Jesus' earlier words to His disciples, "Unless you repent, you will all likewise perish" (Luke 13:3, 5).

William Hendriksen summarizes this Luke 23 passage as "an unforgettable manifestation of the Savior's complete lack of self-pity and of his ardent desire, even now, that the impenitent may repent and be saved."[79]

If you've not yet turned from your sins to Jesus Christ, now is the time.

Man of Sorrows, You have wept
At the grave where Lazarus slept—
Wept to see his loved ones mourn,
Wept to see Your world so torn.
Man of Sorrows, You have wept.
Man of Sorrows, You have wept.

Man of Sorrows, You were scorned—
Mocked as though impurely born;
Taunted as the sinner's Friend,
Yet You stood for the condemned.
Man of Sorrows, You were scorned.
Man of Sorrows, You were scorned.

---

79 William Hendriksen, *New Testament Commentary: Exposition of the Gospel According to Matthew* (Grand Rapids, MI: Baker Academic, 1978), 1026.

Man of Sorrows, You were poor,
Owning but the clothes You wore.
Birds and foxes have a bed;
You had no place for Your head.
Man of Sorrows, You were poor.
Man of Sorrows, You were poor.

Man of Sorrows, You knew loss
Long before the cruel cross.
Good and merciful High Priest,
Share our seen and unseen grief.
Man of Sorrows, share our loss.
Man of Sorrows, share our loss. [80]

~

---

80 Chris Anderson and Richard A. Nichols, "Man of Sorrows" (Church Works Media, 2018).

DAY 22

JESUS' CRUCIFIXION

Mark 15:23; 1 John 4:19

Jesus suffered through the night. Suffered through trials. Suffered through beatings, through mockery, and through the unspeakable brutality of the scourge.

Worn by pain, by blood loss, by grief, He navigated the narrow streets of Jerusalem. Falling beneath the weight of the cross. Unable to bear it alone.

Finally, He arrived at Golgotha. He was stripped naked. His outer garment became the prize of a lucky soldier who won a game of chance (John 19:23–24). Another humiliation. Another insult. Another prophecy fulfilled (Psalm 22:18).

So began the most momentous event in history. And yet, Scripture's description of the event is surprisingly understated: "And they crucified him" (Mark 15:23).

Luke, as was his custom, noted the fidelity of Jesus' female friends, even as all the disciples but John—males—appear to have stayed in hiding. Mary Magdalene, James' and John's mother, and a handful of other women were eyewitnesses of Jesus' crucifixion (Luke 23:49), burial (Luke 23:55), and resurrection (Luke 24:10, 22).

In an encyclopedic article on crucifixion, Henry Dosker details the physical agonies that accompanied death on a cross—the scourging, the nails, the shredded tendons and nerves, the fever-induced confusion, the inevitable dehydration, and the plodding suffocation. He finally concludes, "The victim of crucifixion literally died a thousand deaths."[81]

---

81 Henry E. Dosker, "Cross" in *The International Standard Bible Encyclopedia*, ed. James Orr (Peabody, MA: Hendriksen Publishers, 1956), 2:761.

Jesus' hands and feet were affixed to a rugged cross. While the pain was excruciating, no bones were broken. The Roman torturers were experts at their cruel craft. The cross was hoisted into place with thoughtless efficiency. And Jesus' life began to drip away.

Ken Gire, a master communicator, describes what witnesses would have seen outside the walls of Jerusalem that day:

> Pools of blood beading the dirt beneath the cross. A heavy spike through the feet. Ribs protruding against the skin. Open wounds bothered by flies. Eyes swollen with fever. Hair matted from this morning's thorns. Hands raised to God on splintered wood. A slumped torso, dangling from impaled wrists like some grotesque pendant.[82]

The physical agonies were nearly infinite. And yet they paled in comparison to the spiritual agonies our Savior endured. It was all terrible. *Terrible.*

So, what are we to do with this grisly information? What are we to think? How are we to respond in the face of such agony? How can we move beyond either a sense of revulsion or almost idolatrous reverence for the images conjured in our minds? I suggest two essential responses to the horrors of Calvary. *Abhor your sin. Adore your Savior.*

Look at the cross and abhor your sin.

We only see the cross correctly when we see in it our own guilt. We are as responsible for Jesus' death as Pilate and Herod, the Sanhedrin and the soldiers. *Our* sins put Jesus there. *Our* crimes killed the Son of God. *Our* lust, *our* pride, *our* deceit, *our* rebellion. Scripture reminds us of this repeatedly, each reference resounding like another deafening hammer blow:

> He was pierced *for our transgressions*; he was crushed *for our iniquities.* (Isaiah 53:5)
>
> Christ died *for us.* (Romans 5:8)

---

82 Ken Gire, *Intimate Moments with the Savior: Learning to Love* (Grand Rapids, MI: Daybreak Books, 1989), 114–15.

Christ died *for our sins.* (1 Corinthians 15:3)

How then can we treat our secret sins as cherished prizes? How can we coddle our lust, our greed, our dishonesty? How can we savor the very things that caused our Lord such agonies? How can we rationalize that our sins are no big deal?

Our tolerance of our own sin is obscene. Imagine that my young daughter were ripped to pieces by a stray dog. Imagine me rushing her to the hospital, praying for her recovery, then grieving her death. Now imagine me returning home, seeing the dog that shredded her—and scratching it behind the ears. Wrestling with it. Playing fetch.

It would be *obscene*. I should loathe the beast. I should kill it. I should be merciless. And so should I be with my besetting sins which required the life of the Lord Jesus. Ryle, as ever, is insightful:

> Let us learn from the story of the passion always to hate sin with a great hatred. Sin was the cause of all our Savior's sufferings. Our sins twisted the crown of thorns; our sins drove the nails into his hands and feet; on account of our sins his blood was shed. Surely the thought of Christ crucified should make us loathe all sin.[83]

But there is a positive response to Jesus' suffering as well. Jesus' love should provoke our love in return.

Look at the cross and adore your Savior.

We need to think often on Jesus' suffering for our salvation. But we need to beware of becoming morbidly fixated on His suffering, and even on our grief. Self-loathing is not the first and great commandment. Love is. And if God was deserving of love under the Old Covenant, how much more should Jesus' sacrificial love ignite in us a fiery love in return?

The cross is the crux of the Christian faith. There, God's wrath and God's love converged. There, our debt was paid. There, sin's claim on us was broken and our very identity was changed. There, we

---

83 Ryle, *Expository Thoughts on Matthew*, 392–93.

were purchased from sin as the beloved possessions—indeed, the *children*—of God. There, our hell was borne and our hope was born.

And so, our meditations on the cross should move us beyond grief, to worship, to adoration, and to service. Our sorrow should strengthen our sanctification. Our gratitude should find expression in obedience. And our love for God and others should abound, as 1 John 4:19 says: "We love because He first loved us."

Let the *death* of Jesus, as terrible as it was, transform the way you *live*.

"Worthy, worthy, worthy!" Saints in heav'n exalt Thee.
Lamb, once slain, now raised to reign: Savior, Judge and conq'ring King!
Thou alone art worthy! All was made to please Thee.
Grant that we in heav'n may sing, "Worthy, worthy, worthy!"

"Glory, glory, glory!" We, Thy church, adore Thee.
Called by grace to bring Thee praise; trophies of Thy pow'r to save!
None shall share Thy glory! All shall bow before Thee.
Father, Son and Spirit: One! "Glory, glory, glory!"[84]

∼

Rescue the lost for the sake of His name;
As Christ commands, snatch them out of the flame.
Tell that when Jesus died God's wrath was satisfied.
Urge them to flee to the Lamb Who was slain.

In Jesus' power, preach Christ to the lost;
For Jesus' glory, count all else but loss.
Gather from ev'ry place trophies of sov'reign grace.
Lest life be wasted, exalt Jesus' cross.[85]

∼

---

84 Chris Anderson and Greg Habegger, "Holy, Mighty, Worthy" (Church Works Media, 2006).

85 Chris Anderson and Greg Habegger, "For the Sake of His Name" (Church Works Media, 2010).

DAY 23

JESUS' PRAYER: "FATHER, FORGIVE THEM"
Luke 23:34

We come now to Jesus' seven cries from the cross. As thieves, religious leaders, and passersby mocked Him, the Lord Jesus suffered in "silent dignity,"[86] like a lamb dumb before its shearers (Isaiah 53:7). But when He finally opened His mouth while hanging on the cross—that most rugged of "pulpits"—not a single word was wasted.

He began with a prayer for His afflicters. We might have expected a guttural cry for vengeance, as Samson once prayed (Judges 16:28). The Psalms abound with imprecations He might have called down, even as the "Sons of Thunder" wished for fire to fall from heaven (Luke 9:54). But we get the precise opposite of an imprecatory prayer: "Father, forgive them, for they know not what they do" (Luke 23:34). As prophesied in Isaiah 53:12, the Savior "[made] intercession for the transgressors" even as He died in their place.

We would not blame Jesus if He had offered a prayer for His own relief. His back was shredded, His hands and feet pierced, His face pummeled. Yet, He prayed for His afflicters' pardon. Such a time for such a prayer! Spurgeon shares our wonder:

> Did you notice when it was that Jesus pleaded? It was, *while they were crucifying him.* They had just driven in the nails, they had lifted up the cross, and dashed it down into its socket, and dislocated all his bones.... Ah, dear friends, it was then that, instead of a cry or a groan, this dear Son of God said, "Father, forgive them; for they know not what they do."[87]

---

86 Stalker, 20.

87 Charles H. Spurgeon, *12 Sermons on the "Cries from the Cross"* (Grand Rapids, MI: Baker Book House, 1994), 21. The sermon is titled "Christ's Plea for Ignorant Sinners" and was preached on October 5, 1890.

The crowds' forgiveness was undeserved.

These people were guilty. Guilty of deception. Guilty of blasphemy. Guilty of savagery. Guilty of murder. If ever a sinner has earned God's wrath—and all of us have (John 3:18, 36)—those at Calvary on that dismal day had earned it infinitely more. Their crime was the greatest in all of history, and it cannot be repeated. *Deicide.* The murder of God. As Peter makes clear in the first sermons in the book of Acts, the Jews were *guilty* (Acts 2:23, 36; 3:13–15; 4:10–11). Yes, they acted in ignorance (Acts 3:17). It was a senseless sin. But it was still the most heinous sin of all time.

Contrast the longsuffering of God at Calvary with other accounts of His just wrath. If Korah and his cronies were swallowed up by the earth for opposing Moses (Numbers 16:1–35), is it not a marvel that Jesus' murderers were not? If Uzzah was struck dead for touching the Ark of the Covenant (2 Samuel 6:6–7)—with *good* intentions!—is it not a mystery that those who smote and scourged the Son of God lived to tell about it? If the youths who mocked Elijah's baldness were ravaged by an angry bear (2 Kings 2:23–24), is it not a wonder that those who blasphemed God in the flesh were spared the wrath of an angry Father?

Those who crucified the Prince of Life deserved death. They deserved wrath. They deserved the Lake of Fire. As do we. And yet, Jesus prayed for their forgiveness, and for ours. Indeed, He prayed for their forgiveness *at the very moment He was dying to secure it.* A. W. Pink writes, "It was in view of the Blood He was shedding that the Saviour cried, 'Father, forgive them.'"[88]

The crowds' forgiveness was unsought.

The contrast between the crowds' bloodlust and Jesus' serenity must have been striking. They cried out for His death. They mocked Him for remaining on the cross. The only Person pleading for the crowd's pardon that day was Jesus. They didn't ask for it. Yet, He stayed on the cross to make it possible.

---

[88] Arthur W. Pink, *The Seven Sayings of the Saviour on the Cross* (Grand Rapids, MI: Baker Book House, 1958), 19.

Of course, true forgiveness, in a saving sense, must be requested. If the sinners' hearts remained hard, like Judas', they would bear the punishment of their own sins. But Jesus' desire for their forgiveness was consistent with everything He had taught for the three years leading up to this moment. As Leslie Badham notes, "In his final words the Christ compressed the shining truths his life expressed…. Crucified by hate, Love speaks from the cross."[89]

Let me illustrate this point. Jesus commanded the disciples to turn the other cheek (Matthew 5:39). And now He showed them how. Jesus taught them to love their enemies (Matthew 5:44). Now He did so. Jesus called them to "do good to those who hate you, bless those who curse you, pray for those who abuse you" (Luke 6:27–28)—exactly as He did. Jesus came not to condemn the world, but to save the world (John 3:17). And He was doing so.

Peter's inspired description reiterates the Gospels' narratives: "When [Christ] was reviled, he did not revile in return; when he suffered, he did not threaten, but continued entrusting himself to him who judges justly" (1 Peter 2:23).

The crowds' forgiveness was undenied.

Did the Father grant Jesus' request? It is hard to imagine that He did not. What did that look like? Were the particular crimes of that dark day expunged from their accounts? Or, as I suspect, was there something deeper in motion? Was Jesus actually praying for their *conversions*?

We can only speculate. But I wonder how many of the scoffers—like the penitent thief and the centurion—were moved by Jesus' suffering, *eventually*, to repent of their sins and embrace the Man on the middle cross as their own Savior? I wonder if we won't get to heaven and meet members of that multitude who had once cried out, "Crucify him!" but who later, in answer to Jesus' prayer, silently wept, "God, be merciful to me, a sinner."

---

[89] Leslie Badham, *Love Speaks from the Cross: Thoughts on the Seven Words* (Nashville, TN: Abingdon Press, 1955), 8, 11.

Ah, but perhaps this is no speculation. Peter lays the guilt of Deicide squarely at the feet of the Jerusalem crowd on the day of Pentecost (Acts 2:23, 36). It is very likely that many who heard Peter were among the murderous throng that had crucified Jesus not two months earlier. *When no fewer than three thousand souls were saved in response to Peter's sermon, was it not an answer to Jesus' prayer* (Acts 2:41)? I speculate that *many* of Jesus' murderers turned to Him in repenting faith and will be with us in heaven. Indeed, as MacArthur writes, "In a sense, every pardoned sinner who ever lived is an answer to Christ's prayer."[90]

What could be more gracious? What could be more triumphant?

My Jesus, fair, was pierced by thorns,
By thorns grown from the fall.
Thus He Who gave the curse was torn
To end that curse for all.

My Jesus, meek, was scorned by men,
By men in blasphemy.
"Father, forgive their senseless sin!"
He prayed, for them, for me.

My Jesus, kind, was torn by nails,
By nails of cruel men.
And to His cross, as grace prevailed,
God pinned my wretched sin.

My Jesus, pure, was crushed by God,
By God, in judgment just.
The Father grieved, yet turned His rod
On Christ, made sin for us.

---

90 John MacArthur, "Father, Forgive Them" in *Jesus, Keep Me Near the Cross: Experiencing the Passion and Power of Easter*, ed. Nancy Guthrie (Wheaton, IL: Crossway Books, 2009), 65.

O love divine, O matchless grace—
That God should die for men!
With joyful grief I lift my praise,
Abhorring all my sin,
Adoring only Him.[91]

---

91 Chris Anderson and Greg Habegger, "My Jesus, Fair" (Church Works Media, 2008).

DAY 24

JESUS' MERCY: "TODAY YOU WILL BE WITH ME IN PARADISE"
Luke 23:32–43

Jesus slouched on the cross. A living, breathing scab. His face marred so that He barely resembled a man. His every sluggish breath an agony.

He hung between two thieves, their very company adding to His shame and yet fulfilling biblical prophecy. As Isaiah 53:12 predicted, "He was numbered with the transgressors" (Luke 22:37). He was counted as a common criminal—not only by His murderers, but—astoundingly—by God Himself.

Jesus hung between the two thieves the way He has always stood among men and women—an eternal Dividing Line. Jesus is the great Continental Divide—the One parting people for eternity, the difference between heaven and hell.

Initially, both criminals cried out in disdain, finding some perverse relief for their own pain in hurling barbs at Jesus. Matthew tells us, "And the robbers who were crucified with him also reviled him" (Matthew 27:44).

But over time, one of them paused. Tradition has assigned him the name Dismas. Dismas' life had been squandered. He likely had broken his mother's heart and brought shame on his father. His futile life was reaching a brutal end. And yet, he used his terrible perch on the cross to watch the Lord Jesus, to listen, to reflect. He had heard but one statement from Jesus: "Father, forgive them." And in time—*just* in time—he was won over.

The other thief continued to rail on Jesus: "Are you not the Christ? Save yourself and us!" (Luke 23:39). Though his words might sound like the seed of faith, they were mere mockery, an echo of the jeers he had heard from the mob. Ironically, had Jesus acted on the man's words and saved Himself, He could *not* have saved anyone else.

Dismas had heard enough. He had listened as hundreds of people mocked Jesus from the foot of the cross. Once he ceased from his own abuse of Jesus, he likely listened in silence, not daring to offer a reproof. He had no right. The people were better than him. But *this* man, his fellow criminal, was a peer. Dismas felt some strange sense of duty. He rebuked the other thief, acknowledging their common guilt and contrasting it with Jesus' innocence: "Do you not fear God, since you are under the same sentence of condemnation? And we indeed justly, for we are receiving the due reward of our deeds; but this man has done nothing wrong" (Luke 23:40–41).

And then He spoke to Jesus, offering the simplest of prayers. "Remember me when you come into your kingdom" (Luke 23:42).

Just one sentence, but it contained eternity.

He acknowledged that Jesus is a King. He confessed that Jesus' kingdom is not of this world. He didn't directly ask Jesus for entrance into that kingdom. He deserved no heaven, no mercy, no hope. He simply asked for a remembrance, for a kind thought from Jesus when He Himself entered in. That would be enough.

And it *was* enough. Jesus assured Dismas that that very day—in moments, really—he would be with Him in paradise (Luke 23:42).

Not just in paradise. *With Him.* That was the real grace of it all. Jesus had been the Friend of sinners in life. He was the Friend of sinners in death.

Students of Scripture have long noted Dismas as a trophy of grace. He had no opportunity to do good deeds, no chance at reformation, no time even for baptism. He was a notorious sinner. Hopeless. Damned. Lost.

But he believed in Jesus, and it changed his eternity. When he breathed his last, he awakened in paradise. Not the grave. Certainly not purgatory. *Paradise.* Spurgeon writes, wistfully, that the thief was Jesus' "last companion on earth" but His "first companion in paradise."[92]

The thief's faith is remarkable when you reflect on it. To see in Jesus—despite His blood-crusted face and His naked, tortured body—the true and divine King? To believe, despite the jeering and mocking of the crowd? To see past his own distracting agonies? To repent of a lifetime of evil in a mere moment of grace? It is a marvel. God did that.

Indeed, it's a miracle that *any* of us believe and are saved. Alexander Whyte, the preacher of countless biblical biographies, writes of the hope we sinners should draw from Dismas' story:

> The swiftness of the thief's repentance, and faith, and confession, and pardon, and sanctification, and glorification, is something very blessed for us all to think about, and never to forget; and, especially, those of us who must make haste and lose no more time if we are to be for ever with him and with his Lord in paradise.[93]

The other thief, it seems, died in his defiance, taking his mockery of Jesus to his grave, and to his horrors beyond the grave.

Ken Gire writes, "On either side [hung] two thieves, teetering between life and death, between heaven and hell. Teetering until one, at last, [reached] out in faith."[94]

---

[92] Spurgeon, *12 Sermons*, 28–32. The sermon is titled "The Believing Thief" and was preached on April 7, 1889.

[93] Alexander Whyte, *Bible Characters from the Old and New Testaments* (Grand Rapids, MI: Kregel Publications, 1990), 532–33.

[94] Gire, 107.

Every person teeters in the same way. Jesus, ever in the middle, is the great Dividing Line.

> Whoever believes in him is not condemned, but whoever does not believe is condemned already, because he has not believed in the name of the only Son of God. (John 3:18)

> Whoever believes in the Son has eternal life; whoever does not obey the Son shall not see life, but the wrath of God remains on him. (John 3:36)

> Whoever has the Son has life; whoever does not have the Son of God does not have life. (1 John 5:12)

On which side of Jesus are you?

> *Looking up, I can see Your sympathy;*
> *I doubt myself, but I'm sure of Your love.*
> *Lavish grace was poured out at Calvary,*
> *Securing me for our home above.*
>
> *You are always good, You are only good;*
> *You are always good to me.*
> *Though my eyes can't see, help my heart believe*
> *You are always, only good.*[95]

~

> *Christ will summon His disciples*
> *From His throne beyond the skies:*
> *"You have followed Me through trials;*
> *Follow Me to paradise."*

---

[95] Chris Anderson and Jonathan Hamilton, "You Are Always Good" (Majesty Music, 2014).

"We will follow!" Rise up and say,
"We will follow our Lord!
To the end of the world and age,
We will follow Christ our Lord!"[96]

~

---

[96] Chris Anderson and Greg Habegger, "We Will Follow" (Church Works Media, 2017).

DAY 25

JESUS' COMPASSION: "WOMAN, BEHOLD YOUR SON"

John 19:25–27

We're too hard on Mary. Evangelicals are, I mean.

The Roman Catholic Church prays to her, and it's nothing short of idolatry. But in response, Protestants can almost resent her. And we shouldn't. She's certainly not to blame.

Mary was a godly young girl—likely just a teenager—when she was chosen by God to bring His Son into the world (Luke 1:26–33). She rejoiced in the privilege, though it came with raised eyebrows and dirty looks. Throughout Jesus' lifetime there were off-color jokes about His family: "They said to him, 'We were not born of sexual immorality'" (John 8:41). And these barbs were aimed at His mother, not just Him. She surely felt the sting.

But her famous response to the news of her miraculous pregnancy—the *Magnificat* of Luke 1:46–55—abounds with Bible-saturated praise. She magnified the Lord for the privilege of bearing His Son. She rejoiced in God, her Savior. And after a long journey, harboring in a breezy barn in Bethlehem, she welcomed God's Son, and hers, into the world (Luke 2:1–7). She even tolerated the arrival of strangers in her delivery room—shepherds come to welcome the Lamb of God into the world (Luke 2:8–20).

Eight days later, as she and Joseph took Jesus to the Temple as the Law required, she received a cryptic message from Simeon, an aged and godly man serving there. He rejoiced that God had allowed him to see the Messiah, as promised. He spoke of her newborn's approaching influence (Luke 2:22–32). But he also spoke of the baby's coming suffering—and *hers*.

Behold, this child is appointed for the fall and rising of many in Israel, and for a sign that is opposed (and a sword will pierce through your own soul also), so that thoughts from many hearts may be revealed. (Luke 2:34–35)

A sword would pierce her soul. For over thirty years she had dreaded it.

When Herod the Great (wicked father of a wicked son, Herod Antipas) tried to protect his own throne by killing the infants of Bethlehem, Mary and Joseph hurried Jesus to safety (Matthew 2:13–18). The fact that Egypt was safer than Israel for a Jewish baby boy tells us plenty about the rulers in Palestine during Jesus' lifetime.

Years later, when Jesus, age twelve, had become separated from Mary during a Passover pilgrimage to Jerusalem, she had feared for His safety (Luke 2:41–51). She found Him in the Temple. His principled response to His parents' rebuke was profound: "I must be about my Father's business" (Luke 2:49 KJV). His relieved but rattled mother "treasured up all these things in her heart" (Luke 2:51).

Mary was likely tormented by the thought of an approaching "sword," as any parent can imagine. I love "The Shadow of Death," the painting of William Holman Hunt which depicts the young man Jesus stretching in His father's carpentry shop. His mother cowers before the image of His shadow, which appears to be pinned to a cross. It's an apocryphal painting; no such thing happened. But the dread it depicts in Mary was certainly real.

And now, finally, on this darkest of days, the terrible sword was unsheathed.

Mary stood at the foot of the cross, comforted by the apostle John (John 19:25). We have no record of where Jesus' siblings were. We know they had doubted Him during His earthly ministry (Mark 3:21; 4:3; John 7:5). And we know they would eventually come to follow Him as their Lord rather than as their big brother (James 1:1; Jude 1). But they evidently weren't at the cross. John was.

DAY 25 — JESUS' COMPASSION: "WOMAN, BEHOLD YOUR SON"

Mary was likely widowed. And it was Jesus, her Firstborn, Who felt the responsibility to look after her. At least He had to this point. What would become of her now that His life was ebbing away, breath by faltering breath?

Perhaps it caught Mary off guard when Jesus spoke to her, more concerned about her pain than His own. Selfless to the end. "Woman, behold your son." And then to John, "Behold your mother" (John 19:26–27).

I love this perspective from an anonymous writer: "He, as God, had just provided a heavenly home for a penitent sinner. In the next breath He, as man, now provides an earthly home for His sorrowing mother."[97]

John took that responsibility seriously. He himself tells us the result of Jesus' charge: "And from that hour the disciple took her to his own home" (John 19:27). Giuseppe Ricciotti describes the transaction eloquently:

> In this his last will and testament, the dying Jesus united forever his two greatest earthly loves, the humble woman of Bethlehem and the young man who had heard the beating of his heart at the Last Supper.[98]

With that, Mary basically fades from the pages of Scripture. She and her sons are with the infant church in the upper room, awaiting the pouring out of the Holy Spirit (Acts 1:14). But there's no indication that she was venerated in any sense. She was Jesus' mother. But Jesus was her *Savior*—just like He has been for millions and millions of others.

She is no Redemptrix. She is no Mediatrix. She is not to be the hearer of our prayers. She was a forgiven sinner, just like us. But she was blessed among women (Luke 1:42). She was godly and virtuous.

---

97 An Unknown Christian, *The Gospel in the Seven Words from the Cross: Meditations on Sayings and Incidents Connected to the Passion of Our Lord* (London, England: Marshall, Morgan & Scott, LTD., 1934), 48.

98 Ricciotti, 373–74.

She suffered much, from shame to widowhood to the loss of her beloved Son. A sword pierced her soul.

And on that bitter day, as she gazed up at His bloodied body, she knew that He was about His Father's business yet again.

> *We are His, a cherished bride,*
> *Loved at such a lavish price—*
> *Heaven's justice satisfied,*
> *Paid by Heaven's sacrifice.*
> *Who are we, to be adored*
> *By the Lamb Who took our place?*
> *Held by love's almighty cord,*
> *We are His, a bride of grace.*
> *We are His, a bride of grace.* [99]

---

[99] Chris Anderson and Greg Habegger, "Jehovah's Bride" (Church Works Media, 2011).

DAY 26

JESUS' ABANDONMENT: "MY GOD, MY GOD, WHY HAVE YOU FORSAKEN ME?"

Matthew 27:46

The physical brutality of crucifixion has been often described. Christ was staked to a cross and left to expire by blood loss and suffocation. He was a public spectacle, probably naked. The mocking continued, thrown at Him by an odd alliance of Jews, Romans, and the criminals hanging on each side. The cruelest gibe, however, related to His Father. The chief priests sneered, "He trusts in God; let God deliver him now, if he desires him. For he said, 'I am the Son of God'" (Matthew 27:43). They derided His claim to intimacy with the Father. If God *loved* Him, they reasoned, God would *save* Him. Wondrously, that is precisely what did *not* happen. Instead of delivering Him, the Father forsook Him.

Like petals dropping from a rose, Christ's human companions had fallen away, one after the other. The crowds whom He had fed and healed—who had praised Him when He entered Jerusalem only a few days earlier—were gone. The outcasts He had befriended were nowhere to be found. Most of the publicans and sinners, the healed lepers, the forgiven prostitutes had disappeared. Even His disciples had departed: Judas betraying Him, the eleven abandoning Him, Peter denying Him.

Undaunted, Christ could at least rest in His eternally satisfying relationship with the Father. Don't the Scriptures repeatedly point to God's presence as our comfort even when others fail us? "Fear not," the Bible assures us, "for I am with you" (Isaiah 41:10). Even in "the valley of the shadow of death," David writes, "I will fear no evil, for you are with me" (Psalm 23:4). God had always been with Christ—not just during His human life, but for all of eternity past. The Father, Son, and Spirit had enjoyed eternal, unbroken fellowship. The human abandonment He was experiencing could be borne with silent dignity—as long as God the Father was present.

But He wasn't.

In a cataclysmic breach that we gaze on in awe, the Father forsook the Son in Whom He delighted, leaving the world in physical darkness and leaving the Son in spiritual darkness. Christ, silent through every other blow and abandonment, screamed in desperate, infinite anguish: "My God, my God, why have you forsaken me?" (Matthew 27:46; Psalm 22:1). Scholars call this the "cry of dereliction" or abandonment. Draped in the sins of humanity (2 Corinthians 5:21), Christ endured the terrible reality of Isaiah 59:2:

> But your iniquities have made a separation
> between you and your God,
> and your sins have hidden his face from you
> so that he does not hear.

Stretching back to Eden, separation from God has been among the most grave consequences of sin (Genesis 3:22–24). But at Calvary, the exile earned by our sin was endured by our Savior in our place. Jesus was forsaken by God, suffering the crushing solitude that we deserve. The One of Whom Heaven had twice boasted, "This is my beloved Son!" (Matthew 3:17; 17:5) was rejected by God in sinners' stead. God was, in a strictly relational sense, *estranged from God*.

Faithful Bible teachers have understood Matthew 27:46 this way for generations.[100] I'll note several examples, in part because no line I've written has been questioned for orthodoxy so often as "God estranged from God" in the hymn "His Robes for Mine." My intent

---

100 Philip Yancey writes, "Commentators have observed that the record in Matthew and Mark is one of the strongest proofs that we have an authentic account of what took place on Calvary. For what reason would the founders of a new religion put such despairing words in the mouth of their dying hero—unless that's precisely what he said." Philip Yancey, *The Jesus I Never Knew* (Grand Rapids, MI: Zondervan, 1995), 201.

when I wrote it was to express Jesus' forsakenness in a stirring way—to use *estranged* as a straightforward synonym for *forsaken*. While the mystery of Jesus' forsakenness is surely astonishing, my interpretation is far from novel.

John Calvin writes that Jesus "felt himself to be in some measure estranged from [his Father]," that He had "the perception of God's estrangement from him."[101]

Matthew Henry writes that "God hid his face from him" and "stood at a distance."[102]

Nineteenth-century Scottish theologian George Smeaton notes that the curse "consisted especially in the privation of God ... for the worst ingredient of the curse is the loss of God, or the absence and complete withdrawal of God from a human soul."[103]

Spurgeon speaks of "desertion," of Jesus feeling that "God has withdrawn his comfortable fellowship, and he shivers under the terrible deprivation." He talks of Jesus "mourning the absence of God." He describes "a rupture between a perfectly holy being and the thrice-holy God." And he concludes that "sin is evidently always, in every case, a dividing influence, putting even the Christ himself, as a sin-bearer, in the place of distance."[104]

Most clearly of all, the late R. C. Sproul insists that an actual forsakenness was essential to our salvation:

> Some have interpreted these words to indicate that Christ felt forsaken since He was in the midst of the dark night of the soul He experienced while making His atonement at Calvary, but that He was not truly abandoned by His Father. However,

---

101 Calvin, 17:318–19.

102 Henry, 1769.

103 George Smeaton, *The Apostles' Doctrine of the Atonement* (Edinburgh: Banner of Truth Trust, 1991), 248.

104 Spurgeon, *12 Sermons*, 39–50. The sermon is titled "Lama Sabachthani?" and was preached on March 2, 1890.

if Christ was not truly forsaken by His Father during His execution, then no atonement occurred, because forsakenness was the penalty for sin that God established in the old covenant. Therefore, Christ had to receive the full measure of that penalty on the cross.[105]

The cup which Christ had so dreaded in Gethsemane hours earlier, He drained while on the cross. He consumed God's wrath against every sinner who would ever run to Him for salvation. He didn't deflect or divert God's displeasure against sin and sinners—He entirely *absorbed* it. He bore it all. This is the great doctrine of propitiation (Romans 3:25; 1 John 2:2; 4:10)—that God's wrath has been satisfied by Jesus' sacrifice.

And as Christ became sin for us, His Father moved away from Him.

Because Christ was abandoned, those who trust Him as Savior are welcomed. Because He was cursed, we are blessed. Because He was left in darkness, we have come to the light. Because He was expelled from God's presence, we can enter it through His blood. Because He was forsaken, we will never be forsaken (Hebrews 13:5).

The cost of our salvation is staggering. With your ears attune to Christ's cry of dereliction, yield to Jesus your praise, your life, your all.

His robes for mine: O wonderful exchange!
Clothed in my sin, Christ suffered 'neath God's rage.
Draped in His righteousness, I'm justified.
In Christ I live, for in my place He died.

His robes for mine: what cause have I for dread?
God's daunting Law Christ mastered in my stead.
Faultless I stand with righteous works not mine,
Saved by my Lord's vicarious death and life.

---

105 R. C. Sproul, *The Truth of the Cross* (Orlando, FL: Reformation Trust Publishing, 2007), 120. I could add to this list quotations from Martin Luther, J. C. Ryle, G. Campbell Morgan, John Broadus, J. I. Packer, Jerry Bridges, John MacArthur, and others. Now, they could all be mistaken. But if you disagree with this interpretation, at least understand that it is orthodox.

His robes for mine: God's justice is appeased.
Jesus is crushed, and thus the Father's pleased.
Christ drank God's wrath on sin, then cried, "'Tis done!"
Sin's wage is paid; propitiation won.

His robes for mine: such anguish none can know.
Christ, God's beloved, condemned as though His foe.
He, as though I, accursed and left alone;
I, as though He, embraced and welcomed home!

I cling to Christ, and marvel at the cost:
Jesus forsaken, God estranged from God.
Bought by such love, my life is not my own.
My praise—my all—shall be for Christ alone. [106]

~

---

[106] Chris Anderson and Greg Habegger, "His Robes for Mine" (Church Works Media, 2008).

DAY 27

JESUS' HUMANITY: "I THIRST"
John 19:28–29

Five of Jesus' cries from the cross seem to abound with doctrinal significance. His word to His mother conveys deep compassion. But His fifth cry, "I thirst," can feel rather insignificant.

It is not. The Lord Jesus endured His agonies with majestic silence, and the few words He did speak were pregnant with meaning. So what did Jesus' thirst signify?

Jesus suffered the thirst of physical anguish.

From a strictly anatomical perspective, it is no wonder that the Savior was overcome with thirst. He had passed a sleepless night and been paraded from one unjust trial to the next. He had endured non-stop beatings ever since His arrest, each more vicious than the last. The brutal scourging released His blood on the pavement, on His temporary garment, and now on the cross. He was bleeding to death and certainly dehydrated. He had refused the one drink He had been offered, a drugged wine intended to dull His senses—a miniscule mercy (Matthew 27:34). His body had certainly gone into shock, complete with convulsions. And the sun had beaten down on Him until it disappeared altogether.

Finally, toward the end of His suffering, Jesus drank some sour vinegar, likely requested in preparation for His sixth and seventh cries. Ever aware, He knew that "all was now finished" (John 19:28). He requested the drink and painfully swallowed the few drops of sour wine He managed to suck from a sponge. Once again, a prophecy was fulfilled: "For my thirst they gave me sour wine to drink" (Psalm 69:21).

Philip Yancey notes "the irony of one who had made gallons of wine for a wedding party, who had spoken of living water that would quench all thirst forever, dying with a swollen tongue and the sour smell of spilled vinegar on his beard."[107]

Jesus suffered the thirst of true humanity.

Jesus' gentle complaint of thirst carries theological significance. It is a final reminder of the wonder of the incarnation. Whereas the eternal, omnipotent God has no needs or weaknesses, God-made-flesh endured every human experience except sin. Jesus knew fatigue, illness, hunger, and thirst. His fifth cry draws attention to that fact, and it reminds us that He was not impervious to the agonies being thrust upon Him at Calvary.

Hebrews 2:14–15 tells us that it was necessary for the Son of God to identify with us, *as one of us*, in order to rescue us from sin and death:

> Since therefore the children share in flesh and blood, he himself likewise partook of the same things, that through death he might destroy the one who has the power of death, that is, the devil, and deliver all those who through fear of death were subject to lifelong slavery.

The next several verses, Hebrews 2:16–18, build on those truths, telling us that Jesus had to become fully human in order to be a Propitiation for our sins and a merciful High Priest to meet us in our need and serve on our behalf. All of this Jesus did by taking on a human body—not in a ruse, which He could back out of in a pinch, but with genuine, permanent, pierceable humanity. He was indeed *Immanuel*, God with us. So that He could *die* for us.

And when He laid down His life for us, thirst was one of His many agonies. Jesus experienced the terrors listed in Psalm 22:14–15. He was "poured out like water." His strength was "dried up like a potsherd." His tongue "stuck to his jaws." He was laid "in the dust of death."

Jesus suffered the thirst of eternal hell.

Worst of all, thirst is included in the horrors of hell. Who can forget the torment of the wealthy counterpart to the beggar Lazarus? This

---

107 Yancey, 201.

rich man pleaded for but a drop of water to soothe him from the torments of hell:

> Father Abraham, have mercy on me, and send Lazarus to dip the end of his finger in water and cool my tongue, for I am in anguish in this flame. (Luke 16:24)

No relief was given. No hope was offered that man. But there is hope for us. In this respect, as in so many others, Jesus took hell in our place. We need not thirst for time or eternity.

Throughout Scripture, God uses satisfied thirst as an image of our salvation. Isaiah 55:1 calls out, "Come, everyone who thirsts!" God offers us water, wine, and milk—all "without money and without price."

In John 7, at the high point of the Feast of Booths, Jesus cried out in Jerusalem, "If anyone thirsts, let him come to me and drink. Whoever believes in me, as the Scripture has said, 'Out of his heart will flow rivers of living water'" (v. 37).

The very end of the entire Bible echoes the invitation to salvation offered in Isaiah: "Let the one who is thirsty come; let the one who desires take the water of life without price" (Revelation 22:17).

Best of all, Scripture devotes an entire chapter in John 4 to Jesus' salvation of the Samaritan woman. He masterfully uses water as a picture of salvation. In astounding compassion, He treats this sinful outcast not as one whose filth should be cleansed, but as one whose thirst should be quenched. And He does so—for her, her entire Samaritan village, and sinners like us.[108]

Jesus thirsted that we might be satisfied.

Our salvation is free. We can attain it "without price." But it is only free *to us*. The generous cup of salvation which Jesus has provided for us cost Him dearly. It cost Him everything.

---

108 See my book, *The God Who Satisfies: How Jesus Seeks, Saves, and Satisfies Samaritan Women—Like Us* (Church Works Media, 2016).

Almighty slept—What irony!
Be awed by Christ's humanity.
In cattle stall then violent storm
Almighty slept, first young, then worn.
Almighty slept—Who slumbers not!—
And God as man salvation brought.

The Maker sweat—A mystery!
Be touched by His humility.
By toil fatigued and sin oppressed,
The Maker sweat that we may rest.
The Maker sweat great drops of red
To ponder death in sinners' stead.

The Sov'reign wept—Such empathy!
Be moved by mourning majesty.
As once He grieved at Laz'rus' tomb,
The Sov'reign wept with death-like gloom.
The Sov'reign wept in garden still,
Yet bowed before His Father's will.

The Savior bled—Oh travesty!
Be pierced by Jesus' agony
As Satan raged and sinners scorned
The Savior bled—despised, forlorn.
The Savior bled for sin perverse
To vanquish sin and end the curse.[109]

~

---

109 Chris Anderson, "Almighty Slept" in *Gospel Meditations for Christmas*, ed. Chris Anderson (Church Works Media, 2017), Day 15.

DAY 28

JESUS' TRIUMPH: "IT IS FINISHED"

John 19:30

Jesus' penultimate cry from the cross is a cry of triumph. One anonymous writer calls it "the greatest word ever uttered."[110]

Tetelestai! "It is finished!"

Jesus exerted the last residue of His energy to muster a shockingly loud voice (Matthew 27:50). This was no statement of resignation—*I'm glad that's finally over*. It was a statement of a mission completed, a marathon won, a goal achieved. *I did it! It is finished!*

What was finished? So many things. His perfect life. His agonies. His shame. His abandonment. His conquest of Satan, and sin, and death. His rescue of sinners. The whole ghastly and glorious ordeal.[111]

But there is theological significance to Jesus' sixth cry. The Greek word *tetelestai* is a commercial word, meaning "paid in full." The price of our salvation, the debt we owed, was completely set right by the Lord Jesus' suffering on the cross, culminating in this moment. The debt which sin incurred—every sin of Christ's people, from the Garden of Eden until the end of time—was paid in full. Jesus suffered that much. In particular, He satisfied the wrath of God. Scripture's wonderful word for that satisfaction is *propitiation*.

---

110 An Unknown Christian, *The Gospel in the Seven Words*, 86.

111 On a technical note, the actual payment of our sin wasn't finalized until Jesus died. He couldn't merely have suffered on the cross and lived. Our salvation required His *death*. So He speaks of His work being "finished" just moments before His death, in *anticipation* of it. My thanks to Andy Naselli for helping me to express this appropriately.

Marvel at the undiluted wrath of God.

The word *propitiation* appears only four times in the New Testament—in Romans 3:25; Hebrews 2:17; 1 John 2:2; and 1 John 4:10. Each passage is among the high-water marks of biblical teaching on the significance of Jesus' death. He didn't die merely to display God's love. He didn't die primarily as an example. He died as the Propitiation for our sins—to completely absorb the wrath of God which loomed over sinners. Jesus drained the cup of wrath that awaited us, the very cup He had so dreaded in Gethsemane. On the cross, Jesus absorbed God's wrath so completely that there is no wrath left for the forgiven sinner.

J. I. Packer's chapter on propitiation in *Knowing God* is about as good a description and defense of the doctrine as you'll find. You should read it if you haven't. Here's a taste:

> The wrath of God is as personal, and as potent, as his Love; and, just as the blood-shedding of the Lord Jesus was the direct manifesting of his Father's love toward us, so it was the direct averting of his Father's wrath against us.[112]

So, who was paid this debt at Calvary? *God!* Jesus' offering of Himself was made "to God" (Ephesians 5:2; Hebrews 9:14). Jesus paid our ransom to the holy God of eternity, the righteous Judge of sinners, the Almighty Who is too holy to tolerate sin without punishment. We are saved—*by* God, *from* God, and *for* God.

For that reason, I take exception to a portion of C. S. Lewis' *The Lion, the Witch, and the Wardrobe*. Don't misunderstand me. I love the book. Love it! But it does have a significant flaw. When Aslan pays for Edward's sin—a stirring and beautiful scene—the character who had to be paid for Edward's debt was the White Witch. Basically Satan.

But Jesus didn't pay Satan for our sin debt. John Piper writes, "There is no thought in the Bible that Satan had to be paid off to let sinners be saved. What happened to Satan when Christ died was not payment, but defeat.... There was no negotiation."[113]

---

112 J. I. Packer, *Knowing God* (Downers Grove, IL: InterVarsity Press, 1973), 184.

113 John Piper, *The Passion of Jesus Christ* (Wheaton, IL: Crossway Books, 2004), 34.

The doctrine of propitiation is one reason why false gospels are so onerous. If our good works could save us, God would not have crushed His beloved Son. If we were "good at heart," Jesus could have avoided the cross. If there were *any other way for sinners to be saved*, God would have withheld the cup from His Son. Remember Jesus' words: "O my Father, if it be possible, let this cup pass from me." But it was impossible. The cross was the only way.

The wrath of God, poured out on His only begotten Son, is the greatest example we have of the heinousness of sin. If our sin demanded that God pour out His wrath on Jesus, do you not quake to consider what His wrath will be like for those who have rejected Jesus? If you will not fly to Jesus for salvation, this wrath—the wrath which made the almighty Son of God cry out in abject terror—awaits your own soul. Luther writes, "You must be overwhelmed by the frightful wrath of God who so hated sin that he spared not his only begotten Son. What can the sinner expect if the beloved Son was so afflicted?"[114]

But the cross shows more than God's wrath. It shows us God's love.

Marvel at the unrelenting love of God.

A common error in discussions about Jesus' sacrifice is to miss the love of the Triune God in the whole plan of salvation. There is no "good cop, bad cop" routine in the Godhead. Jesus is not the loving Son Who delivers us from His angry Father. No, the entire Trinity devised a loving plan of redemption in eternity past. Yes, Jesus loves us. And so does the Spirit. And so does the Father.

> For God so loved the world, that he gave his only Son. (John 3:16)

> But God shows his love for us in that while we were still sinners, Christ died for us. (Romans 5:8)

> In this is love, not that we have loved God but that he loved us and sent his Son to be the propitiation for our sins. (1 John 4:10)

Our Savior's crucifixion is the worst thing that ever happened. But it's also the best thing that ever happened. It wasn't a tragedy, but a

---

[114] Martin Luther, "True Contemplations of the Cross" in *Jesus, Keep Me Near the Cross: Experiencing the Passion and Power of Easter*, ed. Nancy Guthrie (Wheaton, IL: Crossway Books, 2009), 10–11.

triumph. And He didn't regret it. He did precisely what He came to do, and in His final breaths, He shouted in celebration. Isaiah 53, which so vividly predicted Jesus' agonies, also describes for us His satisfaction in a job well done.

> Out of the anguish of his soul he shall see and be satisfied;
> by his knowledge shall the righteous one, my servant,
> make many to be accounted righteous,
> and he shall bear their iniquities. (Isaiah 53:11)

Jesus did it. He was successful. He settled the account of our sins. And He was satisfied.

"It is finished!"

> *Praise our Savior, Jesus Christ;*
> *Behold God's once-forsaken Son.*
> *Sinner's Friend and God's Beloved,*
> *By both abandoned, hangs alone.*
> *Dark the sun and dark the sin*
> *Which shrouds the Christ as death draws nigh.*
> *Conq'ring night, our Light and Life,*
> *Shouts "It is finished!"—wondrous cry!*
>
> *Hallelujah! Hallelujah!*
> *Night is over; Light has come!*
> *Hallelujah! Hallelujah!*
> *Praise the Father's glorious Son!*[115]

~

---

[115] Chris Anderson and Paul S. Jones. "Praise Our Savior, Jesus Christ" (Church Works Media and Paul S. Jones, 2008).

DAY

29

JESUS' FAITH: "FATHER, INTO YOUR HANDS I COMMIT MY SPIRIT"

Luke 23:46

Jesus' final cry from the cross settles my soul. He had quaked to face God's wrath in the place of sinners. He had cried out from His heartbreaking solitude, "My God, my God, why have you forsaken me?" But in His final breath, He looked to that same God not as a Judge but as a Father. *Abba*. And He anticipated a joyous reunion. The terrible deprivation of God's tender mercies, Joseph Parker reminds us, "was a *momentary* forsakenness."[116]

It's a happy thought: Christ wasn't estranged from His Father the entire time He was on the cross, but likely only during the three dark hours, when creation itself gave what C. J. Mahaney calls "an atmospheric confirmation of the judgment of God."[117] But we must remember that Jesus' *first* and *last* cries from the cross were prayers. Jesus' first cry was a prayer to His Father for the forgiveness of His killers. And His last cry was a prayer to His Father to receive His spirit in the very moment of His death. On the cross, Jesus experienced and anticipated the fellowship of the Godhead.

In the Son's final prayer, He again found expression for His heart in a psalm:

> Father, into your hands I commit my spirit. (Luke 23:46; Psalm 31:5)

---

[116] Joseph Parker, *Christ's Finished Work: Studies in Matthew Chapters 16–28* (Chattanooga, TN: AMG Publishers, 1998), 207.

[117] C. J. Mahaney, *Living the Cross Centered Life* (Colorado Springs, CO: Multnomah Books, 2006), 91.

In David's original prayer in Psalm 31, he sought God's help and protection as he was surrounded by adversaries. Now, in the mouth of our Savior, the statement serves the same purpose. Jesus was still on the cross, still in agony, still the object of His enemies' derision. And yet, He approached His own death with complete confidence, complete peace, complete solace—as though the world was finally fading away. And it was, at least for Him. He was dying. There would be relief. And there would be reunion. We can almost hear the Father's response to His Son in Isaiah 54:7:

> For a brief moment I deserted you,
> but with great compassion I will gather you.

Two themes are especially remarkable as we meditate on Jesus' final words from the cross. His life was surrendered, not taken. And His spirit was entrusted to His loving Father.

Jesus relinquished His life—it was not taken from Him.

One of the constant themes in the Bible's treatment of Jesus' death is that it was entirely voluntary. Jesus' life wasn't taken from Him. No one had that power, that prerogative, that authority. He Himself chose to lay His life down. He said so repeatedly as He anticipated His death and resurrection.

> The good shepherd lays down his life for the sheep. (John 10:11)

> I lay down my life. (John 10:15, 17)

> No one takes it from me, but I lay it down of my own accord. (John 10:18)

Even the language of Jesus' dying moment underlines His complete control. None of the four Gospel-writers says Jesus "died." He "yielded up his spirit" (Matthew 27:50). He "breathed His last" (Mark 15:37). He committed His spirit to the Father (Luke 23:46). He "bowed his head and gave up his spirit" (John 19:30).

But there is more than death in Jesus' final words. There is hope. And there is life—life beyond the tomb which would soon hold only His body. His spirit was headed elsewhere.

Jesus entrusted His spirit to the Father, anticipating restored fellowship.

A well-known prayer in the Western World, at least in simpler times, was the bedtime prayer recited by children:

> Now I lay me down to sleep,
> I pray Thee, Lord, my soul to keep.
> And if I die before I wake,
> I pray Thee, Lord, my soul to take.

Jesus' final thought before His death was not one of anguish, but of anticipation. He had suffered the deprivation of the Father's favor for a time. But He anticipated a return to the Father's side. His destiny was not hell, for He had suffered hell for sinners on the cross. His destiny was paradise. His body would be laid in the ground, but His spirit was bound for His Father.

The older I get, the more acquainted I become with death. My pastor's role has put me at the bedside of many dear friends as they breathed their last. It is a deep privilege to witness a believer's homegoing. Because of my experience with dying Christians and because of what the Scriptures tell us, I can assure you of this: *Jesus' death was devoid of fear.* There was no gasping, no fighting, no panic. He died because He willed, as He willed, when He willed. He died in complete peace, filled with unshakeable hope.

One of the reasons He became a man was to deliver us from the fear of death (Hebrews 2:15). For now, death continues its grisly work. It has not yet been cast into the Lake of Fire, though its days are numbered (Revelation 20:14). For now, death is still at large.

But death has been tamed. It has no sting for the Christian (1 Corinthians 15:55). It is but a chauffeur, a doorway to paradise, a shortcut to heaven, a fast-pass to Jesus.

In Jesus' death, death itself was *tamed*.

In Jesus' resurrection, death itself was *defeated*.

In Jesus' return, death itself will be *banished*.

Like Jesus, believers can entrust our souls to our Father. We can reflect on the loss of loved ones with hope. We can anticipate our own deaths with confidence, even an appropriate eagerness. As Simeon said, believers can "depart in peace" (Luke 2:29). We can close our eyes and breathe our last, certain that the Lord "our souls will take." There's nothing scary about that. Hallelujah.

Give glory to redemption's Lamb, the Savior of the lost,
Who wore our flesh, then bore our curse upon a cruel cross.
He took the filth and guilt of sin; He took the wrath it earned;
He reconciled our souls to God—the wayward have returned!

We cry "Glory! Honor! Blessing to the King!"
"Power! Splendor!" all creation sings;
We cry "Wisdom! Riches! Thanks unto the Lamb!"
Endless praises to the great "I AM!"[118]

---

[118] Chris Anderson and Richard A. Nichols, "Give Him Glory!" (Church Works Media, 2013).

DAY 30

JESUS' POWER, EVEN IN DEATH
Matthew 27:50–54

An angelic host proclaimed the Messiah's birth. The Father Himself affirmed His delight in the Lord Jesus at both His baptism and His transfiguration. However, as the Lord Jesus suffered and died, Heaven was silent. The angels were surely mute with astonishment.

Yet, a series of miracles announced the accomplishment of our redemption, proclaiming that this was no ordinary man and no normal death.

Beginning at noon, an unnatural darkness engulfed the Earth for three hours, providing a visual manifestation of the spiritual punishment God was executing. Jesus, in Whom there "is no darkness at all" (1 John 1:5), was drowning in the spiritual blackness of man's sin. R. C. Sproul writes, "At the moment when Christ took on Himself the sin of the world, His figure on the cross was the most grotesque, most obscene mass of concentrated sin in the history of the world."[119]

Worse, Jesus was enshrouded in the blackness of God's judgment. Creation matched the mood of its Maker. One songwriter refers to it as "midnight in the middle of the day."[120] Another contrasts the miraculous darkness with the glory that shone at Jesus' birth, calling one "a day like night" and the other "a night like day."[121]

For three hours, this miracle of darkness enveloped the Son's anguish. But when He finally breathed His last, three other miracles shouted of His triumph.

---

119 Sproul, 134.

120 Dottie Rambo, "Midnight in the Middle of the Day" (New Spring, 1978).

121 Dawn Watkins and Dwight Gustafson, "Our Lord, Emmanuel" (BJU Press, 1991).

First, the world shook and rocks were split with a mighty earthquake. A Roman centurion who stood by the cross—an eyewitness of Jesus' peace and of the world's fury—came to faith, acknowledging, "Truly this was the Son of God!" (Matthew 27:54).

At the same time, several tombs were opened, and saints who had died were suddenly alive again. My imagination runs a bit wild here, wondering if Simeon was one of the resurrected believers, and wondering if those sent back to Earth from paradise were a bit miffed by the assignment. Scripture doesn't explain this limited resurrection, despite my curiosity, but it appears to be a foretaste of the resurrection that Christ's work attained for all who believe. Jesus, by dying, conquered death and death's master (Hebrews 2:14; Revelation 1:18). And by Christ's death, Christians live! A handful of believers rose as Jesus bowed His head. But *every* believer will rise when Jesus comes again (1 Thessalonians 4:16).

The most doctrinally significant of the miracles that accompanied our Lord's death was the tearing of the Temple veil. Ever since the Fall, humanity has been barred from God's presence and life with Him. As part of the curse, Adam and Eve were expelled from the sanctuary of Eden. Cherubim guarded the garden, wielding flaming swords (Genesis 3:22–24). Their mission reminds me of Gandalf's bold challenge to the Balrog in *The Fellowship of the Ring*: "You cannot pass!" And no one did.

Even when God stooped to dwell among His people in the Old Testament Tabernacle and Temple, sinners were barred from entering His throne room, the Most Holy Place. A massive veil separated this most sacred spot from the rest of the Temple. Symbolically, the veil was embroidered with cherubim (Exodus 26:1). The décor wasn't random. The cherubim were a nod to the glorious guardians outside Eden. They signaled that God's presence was still inaccessible to sinners.[122] Only one man, the High Priest, could pass

---

[122] For the insight regarding the continuation of cherubim in the Tabernacle and Temple I am indebted to Allen P. Ross, *Recalling the Hope of Glory: Biblical Worship from the Garden to the New Creation* (Grand Rapids, MI: Kregel Academic & Professional, 2006), 115–16.

beyond the veil to offer a blood sacrifice, and he could only do so once a year, on the Day of Atonement (Leviticus 16). Sinners—even heroes like David and Elijah—had no direct access to God. They could not pass.

But all of that changed when the Savior died in the place of sinners. Christ, by His death, removed the barrier between God and sinners that had been in place since Eden. As His life expired, the massive Temple veil tore from top to bottom, signifying that God Himself had cleared the way (Matthew 27:51). It was as though God had commanded the cherubim to sheath their flaming swords and step aside. Access to God was opened for all believers and for all time by the once-for-all sacrifice of Jesus. In an astonishing reversal, God's Son had been banished from God's presence for a time, in the place of sinners (Matthew 27:46). And as a result, blood-washed sinners were now *welcomed back* into the spiritual Eden of God's presence. We now have *access* to God rather than a barrier (Romans 5:2; Ephesians 2:18; 3:12).

More than any other New Testament book, Hebrews celebrates the various and sundry ways in which Jesus' death fulfilled Old Testament predictions. It revels in the rending of the Temple veil. Hebrews 10:19–22 connects the rending of the curtain with the tearing of Christ's flesh. In other words, *Jesus is our Temple* (John 2:19–21), as well as our High Priest and Lamb. As the ultimate Temple, *He* is the place where sin is atoned for and where sinners meet with God. We are invited to "draw near" to God, spiritually entering the Most Holy Place by the "new and living way" which Christ Himself opened by the shedding of His blood (Hebrews 10:22; 4:15–16).

Those who have repented of their sins and trusted in Christ as Savior are welcomed into the very presence of God—*ourselves*, without a human mediator and without an animal sacrifice. We can approach our holy God in prayer, anytime and anywhere. Jesus has made it so. It's a remarkable thing.

The Son was torn, and so the veil was torn. We can draw near to God through Christ.

In Eden's bliss we walked with God
Unhindered by the curse.
Yet we rebelled and were expelled—
Estranged; alone; perverse.
Two mighty cherubs barred the path
To Eden's holy place;
No more could men, now stained by sin,
Behold our Maker's face.

Beneath the Law we sought the Lord
Through sacrifice and priest.
One time each year one man, in fear,
Sought God with blood of beast.
Still mighty cherubs blocked the way
So sinners could not pass—
In curtain sewn, on golden throne,
They stopped the rebel fast.

Then Christ appeared to clear the way
To God for sinful man;
Fulfilled the Law without a flaw—
Our Temple, Priest, and Lamb.
Astounded cherubs stepped aside;
Each hid his flaming sword.
With nail and thorn the Veil was torn;
Draw near through Christ the Lord!

> *In Jesus' name we boldly come*
> *Before the throne of grace.*
> *With empty hand, in Christ we stand*
> *To seek Almighty's face*
> *Till saints and cherubs join in awe*
> *Around the Savior's throne.*
> *With one great voice we will rejoice:*
> *"All praise to Christ alone!"*[123]

---

123 Chris Anderson and James Koerts, "Draw Near through Christ" (Church Works Media, 2010).

DAY 31

JESUS' BURIAL—AND REST
Matthew 27:55–56

It's astounding to think that the events we've considered all took place during a twenty-four-hour period, from sundown to sundown. But that time was fading. The second sunset approached.

The crucified bodies had to be removed from their crosses before the sun melted into the horizon to begin the Sabbath (Deuteronomy 21:22–23). The Jewish leaders who had murdered their Messiah were still maddeningly conscientious about the Sabbath. The Romans, undoubtedly weary and eager to see the turmoil of the day ended, accommodated the Jews by breaking the legs of the men who were crucified to hasten their deaths (John 19:31–32).

Christ, of course, had already died. He suffered no broken bones (John 19:33). It is nearly miraculous that He endured such brutality without even the fracture of a bone. But it had to be so. Ever since God's initial deliverance of the Jews, Passover lambs had to be whole and unblemished (Exodus 12:46).

To verify that Jesus was indeed dead, a soldier pierced His side. The flow of blood and water signified to the professional executioner that Jesus was dead. He wasn't nearly dead; He was gone. Again, a prophecy was fulfilled (Zechariah 12:10).

Jesus' body was removed from the cross. The crucifixion, so grueling and grisly, was complete. The body which had been so often exhausted by days of ministry and nights of sleepless prayer now lay lifeless. As Andrew Peterson so ingeniously reminds us in song, on the seventh day "God rested."[124]

---

124 Andrew Peterson, "God Rested" (Jakedog Music, 2018).

Christ's burial is striking in its simplicity, especially when compared to the funerals of that day. Traditional Jewish funerals were notorious for their length. The deceased would be lamented for days at a time, as we see in John 11. However, Christ's body was wrapped and laid to rest in a hurry—no time for hesitation, for grief, for reflection. In light of the beatings He endured, caring for the body must have been a gruesome task. Still, it had to be done, and hastily, without even a respectful pause. "If the body of Jesus was going to be buried at all," William Hendriksen explains, "it had to be done now, that is, sometime before 6 P.M."[125]

Though Jewish burials were often extravagant, Jesus lacked even the funds to pay for His own tomb. He Who had no place to lay His head in life (Matthew 8:20) had to borrow a place to lay His head in death (Matthew 27:60). Though grief for the deceased was typically shared by entire communities, very few were present at Christ's burial. The eleven disciples were notoriously absent.

Two wealthy Jewish converts named Nicodemus and Joseph of Arimathea were bold enough to ask Pilate for the body and kind enough to care for it (Matthew 27:57–60; John 19:38–42). Both had been only secret disciples of Jesus up to this point, and both had much to lose. Yet, Jesus' death had finally poured iron into their spines. Joseph generously provided the unused tomb, and Nicodemus, the bounty of spices in which they wrapped Jesus' body (John 19:38–42). As Isaiah had prophesied, Jesus associated Himself with both the wicked and the wealthy in His death and burial (Isaiah 53:9).

Besides these good men, several godly women looked on, planning to return after the Sabbath to do justice to their Lord's corpse (Matthew 27:55–56, 61; Luke 23:55–56). Together, the sorrowful company made an odd but fitting portrait of Jesus' ministry: They were few in number. They were both men and women, both rich and poor. They included a respected rabbi and a converted demoniac.

---

125 Hendriksen, *New Testament Commentary: Matthew*, 979.

Even as they sorrowed for His death, they were trophies of the power of His life.

Finally, though Eastern funerals were exhaustingly emotional, often including hired mourners alongside the devastated family, Christ's burial could scarcely be called a funeral at all. Whereas the deaths of great men throughout history are usually spectacles, Jesus was laid in a tomb as a matter of necessity. He, the Creator of heaven and earth, was buried with all the pomp and circumstance of a beggar. He Who wept over Lazarus' death was scarcely mourned.

A great stone was rolled over the tomb's entrance (Matthew 27:60), even as the sun disappeared.

Sundown.

Jerusalem, weary from the tumult, settled into a much-needed hush. Christ's disciples hid themselves away, their fear mingling with sorrow and regret.

Christ's enemies scarcely took time to celebrate their apparent triumph, but instead labored to preserve it. Oblivious that God would use their schemes to trumpet the veracity of Christ's resurrection, they secured the tomb (Matthew 27:62–66).

Jesus' suffering was over.

Jesus' rest had commenced.

Jesus' triumph loomed.

All that had transpired in the twenty-four hours between the Last Supper and Christ's entombment prepared the way for the glorious day we commemorate each Sunday and celebrate each Easter. The stone that was moved by men to mark Messiah's death would be moved by God to mark His resurrection. The sun that hid during the crucifixion would burst forth to announce that He was risen.

Sundown would yield to sunrise; night would give way to day—and for those who trust this mighty Savior, to eternal day.

We have looked in faith to Christ,
Beholding God's atoning Lamb.
He for our sins was sacrificed,
Thus we, though dead, have been born again.

We still look each day to Christ
And by the unveiled view are changed.
The Spirit wields the Truth with might,
Conforming us to the Son unstained.

We will look one day on Christ
When He appears, triumphantly.
That blessed hope now purifies,
Till seeing Him, we like Him will be.

Jesus, Your beauty fills our eyes—
First looking, we were justified;
Now gazing deeper sanctifies,
Till face to face, we are glorified. [126]

---

126 Chris Anderson and Greg Habegger, "Your Beauty Fills Our Eyes" (Church Works Media, 2009).

ACKNOWLEDGMENTS

No theme comes up more frequently in my preaching or hymn-writing than the crucifixion of the Lord Jesus—both its history and its significance. So writing this book was a delight. As always, I'm grateful to be part of a great team.

Joe Tyrpak, who served with me at Tri-County Bible Church in Madison, Ohio, for eight years, first came up with the idea of this devotional back in 2010. He was the one who nudged me over the last year to expand on that initial work and publish it. And he is once again responsible for the artistic editing and layout of the book.

This volume includes over thirty gospel-centered hymn lyrics. It would be impossible to thank the many friends who critiqued those lyrics over the last two decades—but I am grateful for their feedback and for the musicians who have made those (sometimes quite dense) lyrics sing: Greg Habegger, Richard Nichols, Molly Ijames, Matt Taylor, Bob Kauflin, Paul S. Jones, Paul Keew, Heather Schopf, Rebekah Holden, and two friends who are now in heaven, Jonathan Hamilton and James Koerts.

Many, many thanks to the growing Church Works Media team. Abby Huffstutler, my go-to copyeditor, often knows how to say what I mean better than I do. And I rely heavily on CWM's overall operations and get-it-done guy Paul Keew, master filmmaker Peter Hansen, and marketing specialist Scott Ashmore. All of you have helped push this project across the finish line with great efficiency. Thank you!

Finally, I am grateful for all of the opportunities to preach these meditations over the years—at Tri-County Bible Church, Killian Hill Baptist Church, Lebanon Baptist Church, and in scores of other churches, colleges, and conferences. Whether as a pastor, a writing preacher, or now a preaching writer, I'm deeply grateful for the sacred trust of handling the Scriptures and serving Christ's church. I don't take it for granted. All grace.

HYMNS

Learn more and access free downloads online.
churchworksmedia.com

"A Triune Prayer" — p. 34
Words by Chris Anderson; Music by Molly Ijames
© 2010 Beckenhorst Press, Inc. All rights reserved. Used by permission.
CCLI # 5872606

"Christ Is Sufficient" — p. 68
Words by Chris Anderson; Music by Greg Habegger
© 2016 Church Works Worship (ASCAP) (adm at IntegratedRights.com). All rights reserved. Used by permission.
CCLI # 7135352

"Come Quickly, Lord" — p. 86
Words by Chris Anderson; Music by Greg Habegger
© 2008 Church Works Worship (ASCAP) (adm at IntegratedRights.com). All rights reserved. Used by permission.
CCLI # 7146734

"Draw Near through Christ" — p. 148
Words by Chris Anderson; Music by James Koerts
© 2010 Church Works Media. All rights reserved.
CCLI # 7191733

"Every Knee Shall Bow" — p. 77
Words by Chris Anderson; Music by Molly Ijames
© 2012 Church Works Worship (ASCAP) (adm at IntegratedRights.com). All rights reserved. Used by permission.
CCLI # 7191720

"For the Sake of His Name" — p. 110
Words by Chris Anderson; Music by Greg Habegger
© 2010 Church Works Worship (ASCAP) (adm at IntegratedRights.com). All rights reserved. Used by permission.
CCLI # 7146733

"Gaze on the Christ"*—*p. 50
Words by Chris Anderson; Music by Greg Habegger
© 2011 Church Works Worship (ASCAP) (adm at IntegratedRights.com). All rights reserved. Used by permission.
CCLI # 7146737

"Give Him Glory!"*—*p. 144
Words by Chris Anderson; Music by Richard A. Nichols
© 2013 Church Works Worship (ASCAP) (adm at IntegratedRights.com). All rights reserved. Used by permission.
CCLI # 7191734

"God Rested"*—*p. 151
Words and music by Andrew Peterson
© 2018 Jakedog Music (Admin. by Music Services, Inc.). All rights reserved.
CCLI # 7110704

"God Supreme"*—*p. 90
Words by Chris Anderson; Music by Paul Keew
© 2015 Church Works Media. All rights reserved.

"Grace to You"*—*p. 53
Words by Chris Anderson; Music by Heather Schopf
© 2024 Forever Be Sure. All rights reserved. Used by permission.
CCLI # 7247523

"He Was Wounded (Isaiah 53)"*—*p. 72
Words by Chris Anderson; Music by Greg Habegger
© 2010 Church Works Worship (ASCAP) (adm at IntegratedRights.com). All rights reserved. Used by permission.
CCLI # 7191722

"His Robes for Mine"*—*p. 130
Words by Chris Anderson; Music by Greg Habegger
© 2008 Church Works Worship (ASCAP) (adm at IntegratedRights.com). All rights reserved. Used by permission.
CCLI # 7075450

"Holy, Mighty, Worthy" — *p. 110*
Words by Chris Anderson; Music by Greg Habegger
© 2006 Church Works Worship (ASCAP) (adm at IntegratedRights.com). All rights reserved. Used by permission.
CCLI # 7146736

"How Dark the Night" — *p. 42*
Words by Chris Anderson; Music by Greg Habegger
© 2022 Church Works Worship (ASCAP) (adm at IntegratedRights.com). All rights reserved. Used by permission.
CCLI # 7229683

"I Am with You" — *p. 30*
Words by Chris Anderson; Music by Greg Habegger
© 2013 Church Works Worship (ASCAP) (adm at IntegratedRights.com). All rights reserved. Used by permission.
CCLI # 7191770

"I Love the Church" — *p. 22*
Words by Chris Anderson; Music by Greg Habegger
© 2009 Church Works Worship (ASCAP) (adm at IntegratedRights.com). All rights reserved. Used by permission.
CCLI # 7191723

"I Run to Christ" — *p. 82*
Words by Chris Anderson; Music by Greg Habegger
© 2010 Church Works Worship (ASCAP) (adm at IntegratedRights.com). All rights reserved.
CCLI # 6603362

"I Waged a War" — *p. 94*
Words by Chris Anderson; Music by Greg Habegger
© 2025 Church Works Media. All rights reserved.

"Jehovah's Bride" — *p. 126*
Words by Chris Anderson; Music by Greg Habegger
© 2011 Church Works Worship (ASCAP) (adm at IntegratedRights.com). All rights reserved. Used by permission.
CCLI # 7191724

"Jesus, Shepherd" — *p. 11*
Words by Chris Anderson; Music by Matt Taylor
© 2023 The Wilds Christian Association, Inc. All rights reserved.
Used by permission.
CCLI # 7224188

"Man of Sorrows" — *p. 104*
Words by Chris Anderson; Music by Richard A. Nichols
© 2018 Church Works Media. All rights reserved.

"Midnight in the Middle of the Day" — *p. 145*
Words and music by Dottie Rambo
© 1978 New Spring (Admin. by Brentwood-Benson Music Publishing, Inc.). All rights reserved.
CCLI # 49424

"My Jesus, Fair" — *pp. 77, 114*
Words by Chris Anderson; Music by Greg Habegger
© 2008 Church Works Worship (ASCAP) (adm at IntegratedRights.com). All rights reserved. Used by permission.
CCLI # 7075202

"Not to Us (Psalm 115)" — *p. 100*
Words by Chris Anderson; Music (public domain) by George J. Elvey
© 2010 Church Works Worship (ASCAP) (adm at IntegratedRights.com). All rights reserved. Used by permission.
CCLI # 7191778

"Our Lord, Emmanuel" — *p. 145*
Words by Dawn Watkins; Music by Dwight Gustafson
© 2011 Bob Jones University Press. All rights reserved. Used by permission.

"Praise Our Savior, Jesus Christ" — *p. 140*
Words by Chris Anderson; Music by Paul S. Jones
© 2008 Church Works Media and Paul S. Jones. All rights reserved.
CCLI # 7191780

"Reformation Hymn" — p. 38

Words by Chris Anderson; Music by Bob Kauflin
© 2017 Sovereign Grace Praise (BMI) and Church Works Worship (ASCAP) (adm at IntegratedRights.com). All rights reserved. Used by permission.
CCLI # 7085667

"Relentless Love" — p. 58

Words by Chris Anderson; Music by Greg Habegger
© 2011 Church Works Worship (ASCAP) (adm at IntegratedRights.com). All rights reserved. Used by permission.
CCLI # 7191726

"Salvation's Cup" — p. 64

Words by Chris Anderson; Music by Molly Ijames
© 2009 Church Works Worship (ASCAP) (adm at IntegratedRights.com). All rights reserved. Used by permission.
CCLI # 7191787

"The Father Looks on Me" — p. 25

Words by Chris Anderson; Music by Rebekah Holden
© 2015 Church Works Worship (ASCAP) (adm at IntegratedRights.com). All rights reserved. Used by permission.
CCLI # 7191727

"The Love of Christ" — p. 16

Words by Chris Anderson; Music by Richard A. Nichols
© 2015 Church Works Worship (ASCAP) (adm at IntegratedRights.com). All rights reserved. Used by permission.
CCLI # 7237214

"We Will Follow" — p. 120

Words by Chris Anderson; Music by Greg Habegger
© 2017 Church Works Worship (ASCAP) (adm at IntegratedRights.com). All rights reserved. Used by permission.
CCLI # 7191729

"You Are Always Good" — *p. 120*

Words by Chris Anderson; Music by Jonathan Hamilton
© 2014 Majesty Music, Inc. All rights reserved. Used by permission.
CCLI # 7075206

"Your Beauty Fills Our Eyes" — *p. 154*

Words by Chris Anderson; Music by Greg Habegger
© 2009 Church Works Worship (ASCAP) (adm at IntegratedRights.com). All rights reserved. Used by permission.
CCLI # 7191730

"Your Love Returned" — *p. 21*

Words by Chris Anderson; Music by Richard A. Nichols
© 2019 Church Works Media. All rights reserved.

BIBLIOGRAPHY

An Unknown Christian. *The Gospel in the Seven Words from the Cross: Meditations on Sayings and Incidents Connected to the Passion of Our Lord*. London, England: Marshall, Morgan & Scott, LTD., 1934.

Anderson, Chris. "Almighty Slept." In *Gospel Meditations for Christmas*. Edited by Chris Anderson. Church Works Media, 2017.

Badham, Leslie. *Love Speaks from the Cross: Thoughts on the Seven Words*. Nashville, TN: Abingdon Press, 1955.

Bauckham, Richard. "The Trinity and the Gospel of John." In *The Essential Trinity: New Testament Foundations and Practical Relevance*. Edited by Brandon D. Crowe and Carl R. Trueman. Phillipsburg, NJ: P&R Publishing, 2016.

Bridges, Jerry. *The Gospel for Real Life*. Colorado Springs, CO: NavPress, 2003.

Bridges, Jerry. *Trusting God*. Colorado Springs, CO: NavPress, 2008.

Broadus, John A. *Commentary on Matthew*. Grand Rapids, MI: Kregel Publications, 1990.

Brown, John. *The Sufferings and Glories of the Messiah: An Exposition of Psalm 18 and Isaiah 52:13–53:12*. Sovereign Grace Publishers, 1959.

Bruce, A. B. *The Training of the Twelve*. Grand Rapids, MI: Kregel Publications, 1988.

Calvin, John. *Calvin's Commentaries*. Volume 17. Translated by William Pringle. Grand Rapids: Baker Books, 1999.

Calvin, John. *Calvin's Commentaries*. Volume 18. Translated by William Pringle. Grand Rapids: Baker Books, 1999.

Carson, D. A. *The Gospel According to John*. Grand Rapids, MI: William B. Eerdmans Publishing Company, 1991.

Criswell, W. A. *Preaching on the Life of Christ: Sermons on the Epochs in the Life of Christ.* Grand Rapids, MI: Zondervan Publishing House, 1958.

Crowe, Brandon D. and Carl R. Trueman, editors. *The Essential Trinity: New Testament Foundations and Practical Relevance.* Phillipsburg, NJ: P&R Publishing, 2016.

Dosker, Henry E. "Cross." In *The International Standard Bible Encyclopedia.* Volume 2. Edited by James Orr. Peabody, MA: Hendriksen Publishers, 1956.

Dosker, Henry E. "Herod." In *The International Standard Bible Encyclopedia.* Volume 3. Edited by James Orr. Peabody, MA: Hendriksen Publishers, 1956.

Edersheim, Alfred. *The Life and Times of Jesus the Messiah.* Peabody, MA: Hendrickson Publishers, 1993.

Edersheim, Alfred. *Sketches of Jewish Social Life in the Days of Christ.* Grand Rapids, MI: William B. Eerdmans Publishing Company, 1978.

Evans, William. *Epochs in the Life of Christ.* New York, NY: Fleming H. Revell Company, 1916.

Geldenhuys, Norval. *Commentary on the Gospel of Luke: The English Text with Introduction, Exposition, and Notes.* Grand Rapids, MI: William B. Eerdmans Publishing Company, 1993.

Gire, Ken. *Intimate Moments with the Savior: Learning to Love.* Grand Rapids, MI: Daybreak Books, 1989.

Guthrie, Nancy, editor. *Jesus, Keep Me Near the Cross: Experiencing the Passion and Power of Easter.* Wheaton, IL: Crossway, 2009.

Hendriksen, William. *New Testament Commentary: Exposition of the Gospel According to John.* Grand Rapids, MI: Baker Academic, 1953.

Hendriksen, William. *New Testament Commentary: Exposition of the Gospel According to Luke.* Grand Rapids, MI: Baker Academic, 1978.

Hendriksen, William. *New Testament Commentary: Exposition of the Gospel According to Matthew*. Grand Rapids, MI: Baker Academic, 1973.

Henry, Matthew. *Matthew Henry's Commentary on the Whole Bible: Complete and Unabridged in One Volume*. Peabody, MA: Hendrickson Publishers, 1994.

Hughes, R. Kent. "Gethsemane." In *Jesus, Keep Me Near the Cross: Experiencing the Passion and Power of Easter*. Edited by Nancy Guthrie. Wheaton, IL: Crossway Books, 2009.

Jeffery, Steve, Michael Ovey, and Andrew Sach. *Pierced for Our Transgressions: Rediscovering the Glory of Penal Substitution*. Wheaton, IL: Crossway Books, 2007.

Köstenberger, Andreas J. *Baker Exegetical Commentary of the New Testament: John*. Grand Rapids, MI: Baker Academic, 2004.

Letham, Robert. *The Holy Trinity: In Scripture, History, Theology, and Worship*. Phillipsburg, NJ: P&R Publishing, 2019.

Logsdon, S. Franklin. *Lingering at Calvary*. Toronto, Ontario: Evangelical Publishers, 1950.

Luther, Martin. "True Contemplations of the Cross." In *Jesus, Keep Me Near the Cross: Experiencing the Passion and Power of Easter*. Edited by Nancy Guthrie. Wheaton, IL: Crossway Books, 2009.

MacArthur, John Jr. "Father, Forgive Them." In *Jesus, Keep Me Near the Cross: Experiencing the Passion and Power of Easter*. Edited by Nancy Guthrie. Wheaton, IL: Crossway Books, 2009.

MacArthur, John Jr. *The Love of God: He Will Do Whatever It Takes to Make Us Holy*. Dallas, TX: Word Publishing, 1996.

MacArthur, John Jr. *The MacArthur New Testament Commentary: Luke 18–24*. Chicago, IL: Moody Publishers, 2014.

MacArthur, John Jr. *The Murder of Jesus: A Study of How Jesus Died*. Nashville, TN: Word Publishing, 2000.

Maclaren, Alexander. *The Gospel of St. Matthew*. New York, NY: A. C. Armstrong & Son, 1894.

Mahaney, C. J. *Living the Cross Centered Life*. Colorado Springs, CO: Multnomah Books, 2006.

Martin, Hugh. *The Shadow of Calvary*. Carlisle, PA: The Banner of Truth Trust, 2016.

Morgan, G. Campbell. "The Results of the Spirit's Coming." In *Understanding the Holy Spirit*. Edited by G. Campbell Morgan and Charles H. Spurgeon. Chattanooga, TN: AMG Publishers, 1995.

Morris, Leon. *The Atonement: Its Meaning & Significance*. Downers Grove, IL: IVP Academic, 1983.

Morris, Leon. *The Gospel According to John*. Grand Rapids, MI: William B. Eerdmans Publishing Company, 1971.

Morris, Leon. *The Gospel According to St. Luke: An Introduction and Commentary*. Grand Rapids, MI: William B. Eerdmans Publishing Company, 1974.

Ortlund, Dane. *Gentle and Lowly: The Heart of Christ for Sinners and Sufferers*. Wheaton, IL: Crossway, 2020.

Owen, John. *The Works of John Owen, Volume 3*. Edited by William H. Goold. Carlisle, PA: The Banner of Truth Trust, 1965.

Packer, J. I. *Knowing God*. Downers Grove, IL: InterVarsity Press, 1973.

Parker, Joseph. *Christ's Finished Work: Studies in Matthew Chapters 16–28*. Chattanooga, TN: AMG Publishers, 1998.

Pentecost, J. Dwight. *The Words and Works of Jesus Christ: A Study of the Life of Christ*. Grand Rapids, MI: Zondervan Publishing House, 1981.

Pink, Arthur W. *The Seven Sayings of the Saviour on the Cross*. Grand Rapids, MI: Baker Book House, 1958.

Piper, John. *God Is the Gospel: Meditations on God's Love as the Gift of Himself*. Wheaton, IL: Crossway Books, 2005.

Piper, John. *The Passion of Jesus Christ*. Wheaton, IL: Crossway Books, 2004.

Pollock, John. *The Master: A Life of Jesus*. Wheaton, IL: Victor Books, 1985.

Reeves, Michael. *Delighting in the Trinity: An Introduction to the Christian Faith*. Downers Grove, IL: IVP Academic, 2012.

Ricciotti, Giuseppe. *Life of Christ*. Translated by Alba I. Zizzamia. Edited by Aloysius Croft. Milwaukee, WI: The Bruce Publishing Company, 1952.

Robertson, A. T. *Word Pictures in the New Testament*. Volume 1. Nashville, TN: Broadman Press, 1930.

Ross, Allen P. *Recalling the Hope of Glory: Biblical Worship from the Garden to the New Creation*. Grand Rapids, MI: Kregel Academic & Professional, 2006.

Ryle, J. C. *Expository Thoughts on the Gospels: John 10:31–21:25*. Grand Rapids, MI: Baker Book House, 2007.

Ryle, J. C. *Expository Thoughts on the Gospels: Matthew*. Grand Rapids, MI: Baker Book House, 2007.

Scott, J. Julius Jr. *Jewish Backgrounds of the New Testament*. Grand Rapids, MI: Baker Academic, 1995.

Sibbes, Richard. *The Bruised Reed*. Zeeland, MI: Reformed Church Publications, 2009.

Smeaton, George. *The Apostles' Doctrine of the Atonement*. Edinburgh: The Banner of Truth Trust, 1991.

Sproul, R. C. *The Truth of the Cross*. Orlando, FL: Reformation Trust Publishing, 2007.

Spurgeon, Charles. *12 Sermons on the "Cries from the Cross."* Grand Rapids, MI: Baker Book House, 1994.

Spurgeon, Charles. "They Did Spit in His Face." In *Jesus, Keep Me Near the Cross: Experiencing the Passion and Power of Easter*. Edited by Nancy Guthrie. Wheaton, IL: Crossway Books, 2009.

Stalker, James M. *The Trial and Death of Jesus Christ: A Devotional History of Our Lord's Passion*. New York, NY: American Tract Society, 1894.

Stott, John. *The Cross of Christ*. Downers Grove, IL: IVP Books, 2006.

Swindoll, Charles R. *The Darkness and the Dawn: Empowered by the Tragedy and Triumph of the Cross*. Nashville, TN: Word Publishing, 2001.

Swindoll, Charles R. *Jesus: The Greatest Life of All*. Nashville, TN: Thomas Nelson, 2008.

Torrey, R. A. *The Person and Work of the Holy Spirit*. New Kensington, PA: Whitaker House, 1996.

Weatherhead, Leslie D. *A Plain Man Looks at the Cross*. Nashville, TN: Abingdon Press, 1945.

Wilson, J. Macartney. "Pilate, Pontius." In *The International Standard Bible Encyclopedia*. Volume 4. Edited by James Orr. Peabody, MA: Hendriksen Publishers, 1956.

Whyte, Alexander. *Bible Characters from the Old and New Testaments*. Grand Rapids, MI: Kregel Publications, 1990.

Yancey, Philip. *The Jesus I Never Knew*. Grand Rapids, MI: Zondervan, 1995.

YOUR SUPPORT MAKES A DIFFERENCE

Help Spread Gospel-Rich Resources

Your generous donations enable us to continue providing affordable, Christ-centered resources like the one you're holding. As 3 John 8 reminds us, by supporting such efforts, we become "fellow workers for the truth."

Our passion is to serve small churches with limited budgets. That's why we offer many resources, including our songs, for free, and others, like our *Gospel Meditations* devotionals, at minimal margins.

Would you **prayerfully consider making a one-time or recurring gift?** Your generosity helps make gospel-rich materials accessible to believers worldwide.

DID YOU KNOW?

Church Works Media is a 501(c)(3) organization. Your gifts are tax deductible.

Exceptional Christ-centered Resources for the Church

OTHER RESOURCES FROM
CHURCHWORKSMEDIA.COM

Hymn-writer and experienced pastor Chris Anderson unpacks God's amazing gift of music and the role it can play in the life of every Christian. This book considers what Scripture says about the kinds of songs Christians should sing and helps believers choose them intentionally and objectively. It's also packed with extras, including small-group discussion questions!

"A thoughtful book bristling with biblical guidance, designed to help Christians worship God with theological depth and power."

—**Milton Vincent**, pastor, author of *A Gospel Primer for Christians: Learning to See the Glories of God's Love*

God is creating worshipers out of Samaritan women (like us) through the life-changing power of the gospel! John chapter 4 is a microcosm of what God is doing in the world, pointing us to answers for so many problems of our own day, such as racial prejudice, religious confusion, materialism, divorce, and sensuality. Join Chris Anderson on this study through his favorite narrative from Scripture, and find out how Jesus seeks, saves, and satisfies sinners.

"This book draws us into the conversation beside the well to see ourselves and, above all, to see the Hero of the story."

—**Tim Keesee**, author of *Dispatches from the Front: Stories of Gospel Advance in the World's Difficult Places*

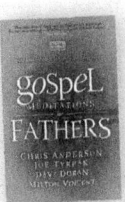
Gospel Meditations for Fathers
"This collection of thirty-one meditations is a must-read for any man striving to fulfill his God-given role as a father. Since each reading is both biblical and practical, it equips the reader to lead family members to greater love to Christ and to God's Word. As parents to four and grandparents to fifteen, Patricia and I recommend this as a fresh resource."

—*John MacArthur*

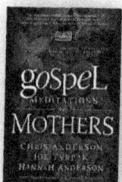
Gospel Meditations for Mothers
"In the midst of busy days and sleepless nights, moms need the encouragement that only the gospel can give. *Gospel Meditations for Mothers* offers powerful biblical truth and guidance that reminds moms of the importance of their labors and cheers them on in their daily tasks. Whether you're parenting a toddler or a teen, these gospel-focused reflections will minister to your heart as you care for your children."

—*Melissa Kruger*

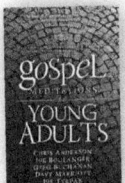
Gospel Meditations for Young Adults
"*Gospel Meditations for Young Adults* is a breath of fresh air for young Christians and for all of us who are raising, discipling, mentoring, or just concerned about them and their spiritual growth and wellbeing. The devotionals are biblical, pastoral, succinct, readable, relevant, and relatable. More importantly, the focus is cross-centered and theological without being forced or trite. This would be a great tool to use in parenting, personal discipleship, group study, or even pastoral counseling."

—*Voddie Baucham*

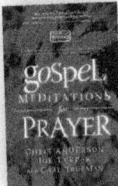
Gospel Meditations for Prayer
"Brief and biblical, these meditations are full of sharp edges. They lead us to pray as cross-bearing disciples of Christ. Yet Anderson, Tyrpak, and Trueman comfort us with Christ's perfect grace for fallen people. So *Gospel Meditations for Prayer* is an encouraging book, but one designed to stretch you."

—*Joel Beeke*

Gospel Meditations for Christmas
"Too often Christmas speeds past us in a blur of busyness and stress, with only the briefest time and the shallowest thoughts given to the Christ that's meant to be at the heart of it all. Give yourself a Christmas to remember by using this profound devotional to pause, ponder, and praise our wonderful Savior."

—*David Murray*

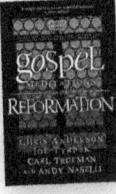
Gospel Meditations on the Reformation
"Theologically rich, thoughtful, and historically rooted devotionals are a rare treat. This volume, which unfolds the theological commitments and pastoral heart of the Reformers, is a unique and enormously helpful devotional."

—*R. Albert Mohler, Jr.*

Gospel Meditations for Women
"Wrestling with guilt and frustration, far too many Christian women are living below the privileges of their spiritual inheritance. The solution is not found in any strengthened resolve of duty, but rather in having souls settled in the blessed liberty of Christ through the sweet enjoyment of the gospel. A union of sound doctrine and practical teaching, *Gospel Meditations for Women* beautifully highlights those unbinding messages of grace that so powerfully ignite joyful passion for Christ and holy living. What an invaluable resource!"

—*Holly Stratton*

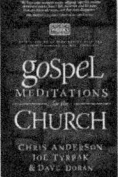

Gospel Meditations for the Church
"We have come to expect meaty, edifying, superbly written devotional entries from Chris Anderson and his team. Here are thirty-one more, and they don't disappoint."

—*Phil Johnson*

Gospel Meditations for Missions
"Can we do missions without meditating on the gospel? Of course not. Yet, how many well-meaning, mission-minded saints go off into the harvest having failed to prepare their own hearts with due consideration of the good news? Too many I fear. *Gospel Meditations for Missions* helps us slow down to consider what is of first importance that we might hold this treasure more fully in our clay hearts."

—*Thabiti Anyabwile*

Gospel Meditations for the Hurting
"These meditations are Word-centered prescriptions that blow away the meaningless Christian platitudes often used to mask unanswerable pain. Until that day when Christ Himself wipes away all tears from our eyes, the Scriptures provide strength, help, and hope in this broken world. Let this book guide you to Christ, the only sure and lasting refuge."

—*Tim Keesee*

Gospel Meditations for Men
"Chris and Joe have co-authored a delightful and helpful little book of daily meditations. This is not one of those trendy Reformed 'the Bible says all men have to act like John Wayne or cavemen with better table manners' kind of productions. Many of the devotions are simply gospel expositions, and those which have a male-specific orientation are on topics like lust, where male psychology is important."

—*Carl Trueman*

Gospel Meditations on Creation
"Jeff Williams is a uniquely gifted human being whom God has put in extraordinary places. What is equally remarkable is how the wonder he finds in our Creator spills into all the ordinariness of the common day. I'd like to be more like that. In this devotional he and his fellow writers encourage us to just be amazed at the beauty and greatness of our Maker and Savior."

—*Keith Getty*

Made in the USA
Coppell, TX
05 April 2025

47962139R00105